Twayne's United States Authors Series

EDITOR OF THIS VOLUME

Warren French

Robert Creeley

TUSAS 310

Photo Credit: *Harry Redl*

Robert Creeley

ROBERT CREELEY

By ARTHUR L. FORD

Lebanon Valley College

TWAYNE PUBLISHERS

A DIVISION OF G. K. HALL & CO., BOSTON

Library of Congress Cataloging in Publication Data

Ford, Arthur Lewis, 1937–
  Robert Creeley.

  (Twayne's United States authors series ; TUSAS 310)
  Bibliography: p. 149–55
  Includes index.
  1. Creeley, Robert, 1926– —Criticism and
interpretation.
PS3505.R43Z67 1978   818'.5'409   78-1863
ISBN 0-8057-7220-0

Contents

About the Author

Professor of English and chairman of the Department of English at Lebanon Valley College, Arthur L. Ford has published the *Joel Barlow* volume in the Twayne United States Authors Series as well as a monograph study of Henry David Thoreau's poetry and has co-edited the two-volume *Works of Joel Barlow.* He has also published his own poetry in various periodicals and in *Three Voices,* and has written the libretti for two one-act operas and the words for a song cycle. Professor Ford earned his Ph.D. from Bowling Green State University and has studied at Gonville and Caius College, Cambridge.

Preface

I make no pretense at unbiased judgment. I decided to write about Robert Creeley only after I had developed an admiration for his work; in fact, I would never have used my time this way had I not first admired him. I also make no pretense of what I have done here. My reading of what others have said of Creeley convinces me of the exclusiveness of my own view, meaning that not very many serious readers of Creeley will agree with much of what I say here; and what I say is, after all, simply the fact of my experience mingling with the fact of Creeley's experience. If you want to learn about Robert Creeley's poetry and prose, read it. Most of it, except the most recent, is available in inexpensive editions. If you are interested in how I read Creeley, then proceed, but keep in mind that these are simply my attempts to explain how I see the work. I understand Creeley's reasons for saying, "As far as I'm concerned and speaking particularly of the situation in poetry, there is *no* correspondence of any interest to me between the activities in contemporary criticism and that poetry I am myself most engaged with."[1] Yet I also believe that readers, if not the poet, can find a correspondence between criticism and poetry, and further, that the correspondence may be both interesting and helpful.

After an introductory chapter, I begin my examination with Creeley's most recent major collection of new poems, *Pieces*, 1969, not just because of the perversity of working backwards but also because I see in this volume the furthest development of certain impulses worked out in his earlier poetry, which I then discuss in Chapter 3 (*Words*, 1967) and Chapter 4 (*For Love*, 1962). Creeley's fiction, which appears in a collection of short stories (*The Gold Diggers*, 1965) and a novel (*The Island*, 1963), is examined in Chapter 5, together with his more recent journallike prose work, *A Day Book*. Chapter 6 surveys briefly Creeley's total production from the point of view of an important but often overlooked preoccupation, concern for form; and Chapter 7 attempts to place Creeley in the larger context of American literature and to offer an assessment of his contributions. I end my examination of Robert Creeley's work with 1976. Although chosen in part for my own convenience, it, nevertheless, appears significant to Creeley as well. That year Creeley published *Away*, a small but substantial volume of new poems; *Presences*, representing his continuing experimentation with nontraditional prose forms; and, finally, his *Selected Poems*, a retrospective collection of poems. And 1976 also saw the separation of Creeley from his wife, Bobbie, an artist and collaborator with Creeley on several of his later works.

I considered using as the epigraph to this book a quote from Yeats, which I first saw relative to Creeley's poetry in an article by Cid Corman, whose contact with Creeley goes back to the 1940s: "We make out of the quarrel with others, rhetoric, but of the quarrel with ourselves, poetry. . . . We sing amid our uncertainties; and, smitten even in the presence of the most high beauty by the knowledge of our solitude, our rhythm shudders. . . . ."[2] In a real sense Creeley is quarreling with himself—in solitude—but the word that seems to apply most particularly to Creeley's work, and increasingly so, is "shudders." Creeley's poetry shudders—almost involuntarily it seems—as one shudders in a sudden draft of cold wind, or with fear, or even with love. But it is important to remember, as Yeats well knew, that a shudder is a physical response to an immediate experience. And so it is with Creeley's poetry.

Finally, another admission—which is painfullly obvious to anyone summarizing the work of a writer still living—it is difficult to assess a writer midway through his career, because he might change everything around with his next volume. Eliot said that each new generation of writers causes us to look differently at the entire tradition. It is equally true that each new product by a writer causes us to look differently at that writer's entire work. Creeley's next book may invalidate, or even make irrelevant, much of what I say here.

My debts are many. First of all I am grateful for the work done by many others who also respect what Creeley is doing. Warren Tallman's observations on Creeley's fiction have been particularly useful, as have others, such as Robert Duncan and Frederick Eckman on his poetry; in fact Creeley is fortunate to have had a number of understanding readers. I found particularly useful Mary Novik's inventory of Creeley's work from 1945 to 1970, a careful and competent survey that saved me personally countless hours of work and that brought a number of items to my attention. Every poet should be fortunate enough to have a Mary Novik. I am also grateful to Lebanon Valley College for financial assistance, to Caius College, Cambridge for hospitality, and to Jeremy Prynne of Caius for helpful commentary, though neither is responsible for anything contained here. And, finally, I thank the libraries of Lebanon Valley College, Franklin and Marshall College, Cambridge University, and The Lockwood Memorial Library, the State University of New York at Buffalo, whose modern poetry collection is a wonder to behold.

ARTHUR L. FORD

Lebanon Valley College

Acknowledgments

The writings of Robert Creeley reproduced in this book are quoted with the permission of their respective publishers as follows:

Presences by permission of *Io*.

St. Martin's, Listen, Thirty Things, and *Away* by permission of Black Sparrow Press.

"The Immoral Proposition," "The Dishonest Mailmen," "A Marriage," "The Wife," "The Door," "The House," "For Love," "The Rhyme," "The Invoice," "The Name," are reprinted by permission of Charles Scribner's Sons from *For Love.* Copyright © 1969 Robert Creeley.

"Water," "Quick-Step," "Song," "Method," "The Box," "A Piece," and "To Bobbie" are reprinted by permission of Charles Scribner's Sons from *Words.* Copyright © 1967 Robert Creeley.

"3 in 1 for Charlotte," "Time," "Having to—," "Place," "Four," "Diction," "The which it," and "Kids Walking Beach" are reprinted by permission of Charles Scribner's Sons from *Pieces.* Copyright © 1969 Robert Creeley.

Excerpts from *The Island* are reprinted by permission of Charles Scribner's Sons. Copyright © 1963 Robert Creeley.

Excerpts from *The Gold Diggers* are reprinted by permission of Charles Scribner's Sons. Copyright © 1965 Robert Creeley.

Chronology

1926   Robert White Creeley born in Arlington, Massachusetts, May 21.

1928   Left eye injured in an accident, resulting in blindness in that eye within two years.

1932   Father died; family moved to farm in West Acton.

1940   Entered Holderness School, Plymouth, New Hampshire, on a scholarship.

1943   Entered Harvard.

1944–   Served as an ambulance driver for the American Field Ser-
1945   vice in India.

1945   Returned to Harvard.

1946   First published poem appeared in the Cummings issue of the Harvard *Wake*, which he helped to edit. Married first wife, Ann MacKinnon, and moved to Provincetown, Massachusetts.

1947   Left Harvard without a degree near the end of his senior year.

1948   Son, David, born.

1948–   Aided by Ann's small trust fund, tried subsistence farming
1951   near Littleton, New Hampshire.

1949   Began correspondence with Cid Corman, later editor of *Origin;* first public reading for Corman's Boston radio program.

1950   Son, Tom, born. Attempted to publish his own magazine with Jacob Leeds, which, after its failure, was reconstituted by Cid Corman as *Origin*. Began correspondence with Charles Olson. Became American editor for Rainer Gerhardt's *Fragmente*.

1951–   Lived in Fontrousse, outside Aix-en–Provence, France, and later in Lambesc.

1951   *Origin* I (Olson issue) appeared, containing "Hart Crane."

1952   Daughter, Charlotte, born. First book of poems, *Le Fou.* Moved to Mallorca.

1953   *The Kind of Act Of* [poems]. *The Immoral Proposition* [Poems].

1954   Early collection of eleven stories, *The Gold Diggers*. Taught at Black Mountain College, North Carolina, from March to July. First issue of *Black Mountain Review*, edited by Creeley, published in March.

1955   Returned to Black Mountain College in July. Divorced from first wife, Ann. *All That is Lovely in Men* [poems].

1956   Left Black Mountain College. *If You* [poems]. Visited San Francisco and settled in Albuquerque where he taught at a boys' school. Received B.A. from Black Mountain College.

1957   Married Bobbie Hall. *The Whip*, a collection of poems from earlier volumes, published in England. "Sing Song," first publication in *Poetry*. Daughter, Sarah, born.

1959   Daughter, Katherine Williams, born. Moved in fall to Guatemala where Creeley worked as a tutor on a plantation. *A Form of Women* [poems].

1960   Received M.A. from the University of New Mexico. Received Levinson Prize for ten poems published in the May issue of *Poetry*. Included in *The New American Poetry: 1945–1960*.

1961   Instructor in English at the University of New Mexico.

1962   *For Love: Poems 1950–1960*. Taught at the University of British Columbia.

1963   Returned to Placitas, New Mexico, north of Albuquerque, to teach at University of New Mexico. Participated in the Vancouver Poetry Festival. *The Island* [novel].

1964   Appointed a Guggenheim Fellow. Received the Leviton-Blumenthal Prize for thirteen poems published in the June issue of *Poetry*.

1965   Participated in the Berkeley Poetry Conference. *The Gold Diggers and Other Stories* [short stories]. Edited, with Donald Allen, *New American Story*. Received a Rockefeller grant.

1966   National Educational Television film, "Poetry: Robert Creeley." Visiting Professor at the State University of New York at Buffalo for 1966–1967. Returned in 1967–1968, 1969–1970, 1970 until present.

1967   *Words* [poems]. Edited, with Donald Allen, *The New Writing in the USA*.

1968   Taught at University of New Mexico.

1969   *Pieces* [poems]. *The Charm* [early hitherto uncollected poems].

1970   Moved to Bolinas, California. Taught at San Francisco State. *A Quick Graph: Collected Notes & Essays* [criticism].

1972   *A Day Book* [journal and poems]. *Listen*, a radio play commissioned by a Cologne, West Germany, radio station.

1973   Edited *Whitman*, a selection of poems. Moved permanently to Buffalo.

1976   *Presences: A Text for Marisol*, prose commentary arising from drawings and collaged sculptures. *Away* [poems]. *Selected Poems*. Divorced from second wife, Bobbie.

1977   Married Penelope Highton.

CHAPTER 1

Two Contexts

R OBERT Creeley said in 1962, "No man can work free of the influence of those whom he may respect in his own art, and why 'originality' should imply, in any sense, that he should, is hard to follow."[1] Looking back over Creeley's poetry contained in *Selected Poems* and over his prose from his recent *Presences* to his early stories, one can see Creeley's work within two contexts—the biographical and the critical. Throughout interviews, lectures, readings, and reviews, Creeley quotes the poets within the critical context with a frequency and passion that suggests a New England Puritan preacher quoting holy scripture, and he also speaks quite openly on occasion of his own past, the biographical context.

I *The Biographical Context*

Dr. Oscar Slate Creeley was head of Symmes Hospital in Arlington, Massachusetts, when on May 21, 1926, his son, Robert White Creeley, was born there.[2] Four years later the father was dead, and years after that the son recalled only dimly the man but remembered vividly the objects associated with him. "My mother even took care of them, or kept them, like his bag for example, or his surgical instruments, or his prescription pads, or, even to quite a late time his doctor's bag still had the various pills and what not in it." "These things," Creeley added, "were really 'my father,' whom I never literally could remember very clearly otherwise."[3] The "literal thing" remains a constant Creeley preoccupation throughout his life and work, but meanwhile, Genevieve Jules Creeley, his French-Canadian and English mother, had to keep the family together.

Shortly before Dr. Creeley's death the family moved from Watertown, where his practice was located, to a farm in West Acton; and after his father's death, Mrs. Creeley became the public health nurse for Stow and later for the Actons. At this time Creeley lost the sight of his left eye as the result of an accident two years earlier. West Acton was a small town twenty-five miles west of Boston: "Low hills, orchard country, chicken farmers and some dairy, and a railroad line through the center of the town, a drug store, post office, town square, watering trough—that kind of environment."[4] Creeley has commented several times on the New England predisposition to make each word count, just as the geographical conditions insist on an economy of natural resources. Then too, growing up in a family of five females caused Creeley to become aware of the signs of human relationships. Since he had to define his own personality without the context of a male-oriented world, he noted closely those small gestures and innuendoes "manifest in women's conduct,"[5] signs used later in his own poetry and fiction of human relationships. But rural New England also provided Creeley with that presence of life noted by many other writers of the region. "I could go out into those woods and feel completely open. I mean, all the kinds of dilemma that I would feel sometimes would be resolved by going out into the woods, and equally that immanence, that spill of life all around, like the spring in New England where you get that crazy water, the trickles of water every place, the moisture, the shyness, and the particularity of things. . . ."[6]

In 1940 Creeley's sister, Helen, told Mrs. Creeley of a small, private school in Plymouth, New Hampshire, and that fall Creeley entered Holderness School on a scholarship. While there he worked on all the school publications, including the school newspaper; the yearbook, which he co-edited; *The Holderness Bull,* of which he became first editor in 1943; and *The Dial,* the literary magazine, which he served as editor-in-chief. Despite these interests in writing, Creeley considered seriously the study of veterinary science—he speaks of his early love for animals—and even received scholarships for this study from Amherst and the University of Pennsylvania. Finally, however, in the summer of 1943 he entered Harvard under an accelerated, wartime program, thus beginning a course that would lead him eventually into the middle of a poetic revolution.

At Harvard Creeley studied under such teachers as Gordon McCreary, F. O. Matthiessen, Harry Levin, and Delmore Schwartz; and he counted among his friends John Hall, John Hawkes, Mitchell Goodman, Kenneth Koch, and Seymour Lawrence. But these were the war years, upsetting at best. Creeley recalls: "I can remember the constant shift and change of the educational form trying to deal with that stretch. . . . A very chaotic time indeed."[7] Less than two years after entering Harvard, Creeley left for a year's work as an ambulance driver with the American Field Service in the India-Burma theater.

Following his return to the states in late 1945, Creeley married his first wife, Ann MacKinnon, and in 1946 reentered Harvard, which he found had changed, partly because of changes in society following the war and partly because of changes within himself.

Everyone was looking for where it was happening and desperately wanted to be accepted by it, because frankly the society as it then was, coming back from the war and realizing home and mother just wasn't, no matter how lovely, any great possibility. And equally the fade-out of the whole sense of being *professional:* trying to become a doctor, a lawyer, the value of one's life as a progression toward some attention was gone because the war demonstrated that no matter how much you tried, as Morganthau said: *facts have their own dynamic*—and this could never be anticipated by any form of adjustment."[8]

Friends who shared this feeling of dissociation introduced Creeley to alternatives to what then appeared as the main stream of American values. He had experienced marijuana while in India. In the literature currently being produced he saw Henry Miller, D. H. Lawrence, and Hart Crane as models rather than W. H. Auden, because "they were the people who kept saying that . . . you really have access to your feelings and can really use them as a demonstration of your own reality. You can write directly from that which you feel."[9] But it was jazz that occupied much of Creeley's time during the late 1940s. The relationship between jazz and his own developing ideas about poetry is discussed later in this chapter; it is sufficient here to repeat Creeley's own words: "This is what I was doing from 1946 to 1950. I was frankly doing almost nothing else but sitting around listening to records."[10] Creeley nevertheless did find time to help edit the Cummings' issue (Spring 1946) of the Harvard *Wake*, which had been newly formed as an alternative to the more traditional *Advocate* and which contained his first published poem, "Return."

Meanwhile Creeley and Ann had moved in 1946 to Provincetown, then an artists' colony, where they lived on Ann's small trust fund

and from which Creeley commuted by boat each day to his classes at
Harvard, usually arriving drunk, liquor being served during the
trip. While he went through the mechanics of education in his
classes, he received an alternative education in Provincetown
through his acquaintance with Slater Brown, who had been a writer
and friend of Hart Crane and Cummings. He was in fact the model
for B in Cummings' *The Enormous Room.* At that time Brown was
drinking heavily and was almost totally ignored by his contemporaries, but he provided Creeley an audience for his own ideas
about writing. As Creeley has said, "He paid me the respect of
taking me seriously in my own intentions."[11] Other writers such as
William Carlos Williams and Charles Olson were to do this later, as
Creeley himself has done for others, but this was Creeley's first
sustained and serious literary association.

The combination of drinking, commuting, dissatisfaction with
existing conditions, and a growing realization that his path lay outside traditional academic avenues, aided by a dean's suggestion,
caused Creeley to leave Harvard during the last semester of his
senior year. He and Ann moved first to Truro, also on Cape Cod,
and then in 1948 to a farm one-half mile east of Barrett's Crossing,
near Littleton, New Hampshire, where they hoped to do subsistence farming supplemented by Ann's trust income of $215 a month.
The location was beautiful, but the farm was run down, making it
too expensive to maintain successfully. Everything needed repair,
but despite the constant concern about money, Creeley here began
to build certain concepts and relationships that have remained with
him. In December 1949, he heard by chance Cid Corman's radio
program out of Boston, "This Is Poetry," and wrote to him. The
immediate result was Creeley's first public reading in January 1950,
but the more lasting result was a continuing friendship and correspondence with Corman.

Early in 1950 Creeley and a friend, Jacob Leed, decided to publish a magazine as an alternative to those being published at the
time. They simply wrote to everyone they could think of and received replies from William Carlos Williams, Vincent Ferrini, Paul
Blackburn, Paul Goodman, Samuel French, Jacques Prevert, William Bronk, Corman, Byron Vazakas, W. J. Smith, Donald
Paquette, and Denise Levertov.[12] Although the magazine was
never published, because Leed's handpress proved unworkable,
much of the material collected was incorporated into the first issue

of Cid Corman's *Origin*, the first poetry magazine to give voice to the Pound-Williams-Olson group of the early 1950s and the forerunner of Creeley's own important *Black Mountain Review*. The same year saw a correspondence begin that was crucial both to Creeley and to the course of a significant body of American poetry. When Ferrini had sent some of Charles Olson's poetry to Creeley for his magazine, Creeley wrote directly to Olson, giving him his reaction to the material. Olson responded with a letter dated April 24, 1950, and a correspondence began that ran to thousands of letters, including portions later published as Olson's seminal essay, "Projective Verse," and *Mayan Letters*. At about this time, too, Creeley, always a dedicated letter writer, corresponded with Pound and Williams; Williams particularly gave Creeley specific help and encouragement.

Unable to sustain themselves in New Hampshire, the Creeleys took the advice of Creeley's friend from Harvard, Mitchell Goodman, and his wife, the poet Denise Levertov, and moved to southern France in May 1951. The Goodmans had assured the Creeleys that they could live on their small income in France; but soon after arriving in Fontrousse and then moving to Lambesc, inflation depleted their reserves and the general anti-American climate proved discouraging. Meanwhile, however, Creeley's literary career began to develop. *Origin* I contained "Hart Crane," the first poem of the later collected *For Love: Poems 1950–1960*; *Origin* II published four poems, three stories, and some criticism; and *New Directions* No. 13 published five stories together with an introduction by Charles Olson. Creeley had been the American editor (1950–1951) for Rainer Gerhardt's short-lived magazine *Fragmente* which published in its second and last issue (1952) two stories, "The Lover" and "The Seance," in translations by Gerhardt. Then too, in October 1952, Richard Emerson and Frederick Eckman published Creeley's first volume of poems, *Le Fou*, as a chapbook in the Golden Goose series.

Meanwhile, Creeley's correspondence brought him another fateful change of place. Martin Seymour-Smith, a British poet, was tutoring Robert Graves' son on Mallorca when Creeley wrote to him concerning one of the Englishman's poems. In the ensuing exchange of letters, Creeley mentioned his dissatisfaction with France, and following a visit by Seymour-Smith and his wife, the Creeleys moved to Mallorca. From November 1952 until October

1954 they lived in Banyalbufar on the northeast coast of the Spanish island and then moved to Bonanova, a town outside the capital of Palma, until July 1955. These years provided much of the material for his novel, *The Island*, but more importantly, they saw Creeley establish his own press, The Divers Press, expand the range of his contacts, and finally, begin the *Black Mountain Review*, which gave both a voice and a direction to many young writers of the time and which eventually brought Creeley to Black Mountain College.

Creeley and Seymour-Smith had begun a cooperative publishing venture in the fall of 1952 under the name of the Roebuck Press. Soon, however, Creeley realized that the two disagreed fundamentally, and so he and Ann changed the name to the Divers Press, consequently producing a number of works that would not otherwise have been published. Among these volumes were several by Creeley—*The Kind of Act of* (1953), his second collection of poems; *The Gold Diggers* (1954), an early collection of eleven stories; and *A Snarling Garland of Xmas Verses* (1954), a collection of five poems—and a number of books by other writers, including Paul Blackburn, Olson, Larry Eigner, Irving Layton, Seymour-Smith, Katue Kitasono, and Robert Duncan. During these years at Mallorca, Creeley continued his extensive correspondence with Olson, although the two had never met. Creeley was beginning to feel the need for a new magazine related more to his own intentions at the time, and Olson wanted a magazine that could in part help publicize the fact that Black Mountain College, headed by Olson, still existed. Since Creeley had access on Mallorca to an inexpensive press, *Black Mountain Review* was born; and despite its circulation of only four or five hundred copies, the review from its first issue in the spring of 1954 to the seventh and final issue in 1957 provided a nexus for new poets emerging in the 1950s, while publishing a wide range of talents and personalities. Today it is looked upon as the most important and one of the most coherent little magazines of that era.

Further, it finally brought Olson and Creeley together. Shortly after the publication of the first issue of *Black Mountain Review*, Creeley left his family in Mallorca to accept Olson's invitation to teach at Black Mountain College, remaining there from March to July in 1954 before returning to Mallorca for one more year. In 1955 he ended his marriage to Ann and left Mallorca in July, subsequently teaching for approximately a year at the college before departing for the west coast early in 1956. The story of Black Mountain College and of Creeley's role there is told by Martin Duberman in *An Exploration in Community: Black Mountain*. Since the Black Mountain experience is discussed later in this chapter, it is sufficient here to say that this unconventional college, which practiced the arts rather than merely talking about them, widened still further Creeley's circle of friends and his interests in the other arts as well.

After leaving Black Mountain College, Creeley made his way first to Albuquerque, New Mexico, and then to San Francisco, where he found the San Francisco "Renaissance" emerging from the literary underground. Here he met poets such as Allen Ginsberg, with whom he had been corresponding for some time, and Gary Snyder, Philip Whalen, Kenneth Rexroth, and Philip Lamantia. The final issue of *Black Mountain Review*, No. 7, was put together in San Francisco and included enough material from this group to be seen as a major document of the "beat" movement. Despite his involvement with the group (David Ossman's important collection of radio interviews, *The Sullen Art*, contains on its cover a photograph of Creeley intently reading his poems to a small group of equally intent friends), Creeley returned in the summer of 1956 to Albuquerque, where he found a job teaching French, English, history, and later Latin in a day school for boys. Here he met, in January 1957, his second wife, Bobbie Louise Hall and began work on an M. A. at the University to New Mexico in the summer of 1957. Because he needed a B. A. to begin work on the master's degree and because he had never finished his degree at Harvard, Olson simply awarded him a B. A. from Black Mountain on the delightfully perceptive and typically nonbureaucratic basis of his having taught the courses.

From 1956 to 1959 Creeley continued to work at the boys' school in Albuquerque, interrupted by a summer 1958, stay in Mexico and followed by a two year (1959–1961) job as a tutor on a Guatemalan *finca* or plantation. In 1960 he received his M. A. from the University of New Mexico, and the following year began a new academic career, which he has continued to the present, when he became an instructor in English at New Mexico. During the last half of the 1950s, Creeley continued to write, primarily poetry, with his reputation gradually emerging from the literary underground. As Mary Novik's *Inventory* of his publications clearly indicates, Creeley, who began by publishing in a succession of little-known and short-lived magazines such as *Goad*, *Gryphon*, *Four Winds*, and in Canadian magazines such as *Contact* and *CIV/n*, gradually emerged from important but limited circulation magazines such as *Origin, Golden Goose*, and *Black Mountain Review* to national recognition in *Poetry*, which published "Sing Song" in its August 1957 issue, and finally to inclusion in Donald Allen's significant 1960 anthology, *New American Poetry: 1945–1960*. The publication of Creeley's books followed a similar course. As mentioned earlier, his first book of poems, *Le Fou*, was published by Golden Goose, and Creeley's own Divers Press published the second book of poems, *The Kind of Act Of*, and the first collection of his stories, *The Gold Diggers*. The third and fourth books of poems, *The Immoral Proposition* (1953) and *All That Is Lovely in Men* (1955), were published by Jonathan Williams; the fifth, *If You* (1956), by the Porpoise Bookshop in San Francisco; the sixth, *The Whip* (1957), by Migrant Books in England; and the seventh, *A Form of Women* (1959), by Jargon Books. Creeley's reputation remained somewhat limited until the publication of the first collected trade edition of his poems, *For Love: Poems 1950–1960* (1962), by Scribner's, followed by his novel, *The Island* (1963); *The Gold Diggers and Other Stories* (1965); two additional collections of poems, *Words* (1965) and *Pieces* (1969); and a collection of poems plus a long journal entry, *A Day Book* (1972), all by Scribner's. In 1976 Black Sparrow brought out a short collection of new poems, *Away;* and Scribner's published *Presences*, a "text" for a group of photographs of Marisol's drawings and collaged sculptures as well as, most significantly, *Selected Poems*, poems from Creeley's entire career. In addition, most of Creeley's work has been published in England by the important publishing house of John Calder (later by Calder and Boyars). While Creeley was published throughout the sixties by these prestigious houses, he continued to produce or have produced many small, limited editions of his works, and continued to publish in ephemeral and little known magazines. In other words, while publishing in establishment sources, he continued to support and use the many nonestablishment magazines and presses; in fact, he appears in the 1970s to be using these presses, especially Black Sparrow and Four Seasons, almost exclusively. Perhaps now that his name is secure, he can use a press that exerts little or no control over what he publishes; at any rate, as Novik says, "His latest writings are as hard to find as his earliest."[13]

During the 1960s and into the 1970s, Creeley taught at the University of New Mexico, the University of British Columbia, San

Francisco State College, and finally the State University of New York at Buffalo, where he is professor of English. This period saw Creeley continue to wrestle with the demands of his own poetry, as he wrote, attended conferences, gave interviews and readings of his own poetry, and increasingly served, not always comfortably, as focus for the emerging interests and talents of younger poets. Creeley's poetry is essentially private, and he himself has consistently sought the relatively remote locus. Even during the turbulent sixties, when many writers concentrated on the antiwar effort, Creeley could not, like so many others, use his poetry as part of the movement. Personally he opposed the war and donated time and talent to its opposition, but as he said in a 1965 interview with Linda Wagner, "I'm not often able to involve a political context in my writing."[14] Four years later he elaborated on that thought:

One dilemma for me in the political context has been the insistent didacticism of attitude, the locked mind that enters almost immediately with any political statement, the insistent rhetoric which places the words in an extraordinarily locked condition. Particularly writers, such as Olson or Ginsberg or Levertov or Duncan or Bly, find it possible to use this condition of feeling as material, and to discover a language that can be this material. Myself, I haven't been able to do that. I've done a lot—not a lot—I've put my own commitments on the line, I think, by holding draft cards and by reading for the Resistance and I've had no intention not to state myself politically, but this hasn't entered my poetry. It's almost as if I've given so damn much to that idiot war I'm damned if I'm going to give it my experience of words.[15]

For Creeley, all language is in a sense a political act, and the poet's greatest responsibility is to the integrity of his language. The single most consistent concern of Creeley the writer has been this obsession with getting the word precisely right, in terms of the demands of language and in terms of his own insistences. Increasingly, the "things" of experience, such as the physical reminders of his father, have been not so much replaced as augmented by the physical reality of the word, the word-as-thing of *Pieces* and beyond.

Two events mark 1976 as a possible watershed year for Robert Creeley. In that year he published his *Selected Poems*, a collection of poems from *For Love* through several recent previously uncollected poems. Here for the first time the reader can see the range of Creeley's poetry in one easily accessible volume. In that year too,

Creeley separated from his second wife, Bobbie, who had provided a source for much of his poetry over the past twenty years.[16] The effect of both events will be determined later; for now Creeley continues to teach and to write.

II *The Critical Context*

Fortunately, many of Creeley's essays, reviews, and interviews are easily accessible in three volumes: *A Quick Graph* (1970), *A Sense of Measure* (1973), and *Contexts of Poetry: Interviews 1961–1971*, which form a lucid, consistent statement of Creeley's thoughts on his and others' poetics since the late 1940s. A brief, tentative summary of what he thinks happens in a poem will be useful at this point, and an examination of his relationship with certain key ideas of several other poets should both clarify and reveal the depth and awareness of those ideas, the point being that Creeley knows what he wants.

First the summary. From the early years when he first became aware of Williams, Pound, and Olson through exchanges of correspondence until the present, Creeley has insisted that a poem is more than a recording of external facts (crucial as the precision and substantiality of that record is); a poem is the play of experience on the poet involving both the external fact and the internal emotion with the emotion given form through the finished poem. The implications are clear: the poem is more than ego, it is more than image, and it has little to do with metaphor. The "point" of a poem is not what it suggests beyond itself but rather what it is, and the form (both in its visual arrangement and—more importantly—in its arrangement of sounds) is given to it by its own necessities, that is, by what the poet feels and thinks is needed to present the poem. The form that a poem takes then never precedes the poem itself but rather comes from the demands of the poem as it is in the process of being uttered. This organic concept of poetry is not new with Creeley, of course, or for that matter with Olson and Williams (for the modern American poet it goes back through Whitman to Coleridge), but Creeley does insist that the poem must be true to a "sense of measure." In other words, the poem must be free from a preconceived rhythmical structure, while at the same time adhering to certain rhythmical patterns within itself, which may involve, in fact, similar and dissimilar sounds within and between lines, textures of words and sounds, indeed textures of ideas themselves. The sense of measure then is the sense of the poem's measure as it is being created. In an exchange of letters with Olson in the late forties, Creeley had written "Form is never more than an extension of content"; and in an interview with Linda Wagner in 1965 he said of that statement: "I would now almost amend the statement to say, 'Form is what happens.' "[17] Earlier than that, in 1961, he had said in a slightly less succinct mood: "The poem is not a signboard, pointing to a content ultimately to be regarded; but is, on the contrary, a form inhabited by intelligence and feeling. It is the way a poem speaks, not the matter, that proves its effects. . . ."[18]

Such a summary is necessarily simplistic. As discussed in his substantial critical material, this method is worked out in detail, and as developed in his poetry it produces subtlety and modulation. The interchange of certain important ideas that existed between Creeley and Williams or Olson and that continues to exist between Creeley and a number of his contemporaries will expand and illuminate this method.

III   *The Projectivist Movement*

Creeley has long been aware that he is part of a definable tradition in the American poetry of this century—so long as "tradition" is thought of in general terms and so long as it recognizes crucial distinctions among its members. The tradition most visible to the general public has been the Eliot-Stevens tradition supported by the intellectual probings of the New Critics in the 1940s and early 1950s. Parallel to that tradition has been the tradition Creeley identifies with, the Pound-Olson-Zukofsky-Black Mountain tradition—what M. L. Rosenthal calls "The Projectivist Movement."[19]

In 1965 Creeley published several articles in which he looked back upon the poetic situation of the 1940s. He referred to the models held up for the young: Auden, "wherein a socially based use of irony became the uselessly exact vigor of repetitive verse patterns"; and Stevens, "whose mind one respected, in the questions it realized, but again whose use of poetry had fallen to the questionable fact of a device."[20] Then in reaction to Robert Duncan's essay of 1961, "Ideas of the Meaning of Form," which described the academic rigidity of the period, he said: "Confronting such *rule*, men were driven back upon the particulars of their own experience, the literal *things* of an immediate environment, wherewith to acknowledge the possibilities of their own lives."[21] And finally, he commented on the impact that Olson's "Projective Verse" had on young poets when it was published in 1950: "It was an excitement which many of us shared, because what confronted us in 1950 was a closed system indeed, poems patterned upon exterior and traditionally accepted models. The New Criticism of that period was dominant and would not admit the possibility of verse considered as an 'open field.' "[22] Even then the course was clear. In a 1951 review of Olson's *Y & X* he said, "Any movement poetry can now make beyond the achievement of Pound, Williams, et al, must make use of the fact of their work, and, further, of what each has stressed as the main work now to be done."[23]

IV *Pound and Williams*

Looming over all other poets of this century is Ezra Pound, because this poet, Creeley believes, by his teaching and by his example, developed new possibilities for American poets. As Chaucer and Spenser before him, Pound extended the possibilities of poetry and achieved a level of technical excellence that will provide a poetic standard for many years to come. Pound showed Creeley in his early years—and continued to remind him from then on—that he must look closely and listen closely, that the precision of the perception and the movement of the line are crucial. "It was impossible to avoid the insistence he put on *precisely* how the line *goes,* how the word *is,* in its context, what *has been* done, in the practice of verse—and what *now* seems possible to do. It was, then, a *measure* he taught—and a measure in just that sense William Carlos Williams insisted upon."[24]

But, pervasive as Pound is in this century, for Creeley the most immediately useful poets were Williams and Charles Olson. Dr. Williams of Rutherford, New Jersey, general practitioner and poet, has achieved sainthood among many poets of Creeley's generation. He was a good and compassionate man who wrote detailed letters of advice and encouragement to unknown poets. He was an honest man who stayed with his people and with his material, an American in the deepest, nonchauvinistic use of that word, reflecting an almost mythic sense of the land and an intuitive awareness—though he worked hard at perfecting it—of the unique speech patterns of the people and therefore an awareness of the people themselves. He was also a man who had been young with Pound, and Marianne Moore, and H. D., a man who could criticize Pound and still assume his friendship because they were equal. He was a man unrecognized as genius by the larger public and therefore savored even more by those who did recognize him. And, finally, he was a man in whose poetry Creeley recognized certain impulses of his own as yet unshaped verse. Little wonder Creeley quoted him then and continues to quote him with reverence.

Williams urged, by precept and by example, that American poetry turn to an authenticity of utterance based on an authenticity of experience, an authenticity found in the early explorers and settlers of this country, but since then largely lost. Columbus, Bradford, Boone experienced directly the virgin continent and captured that immediacy; whereas others only wrote about it, removed from the experience. Williams, in his account of America's past, *In the American Grain*, reflects on what Boone must have experienced when looking down upon a Kentucky valley for the first time, and then compares that to John Filson's "silly phrases and total disregard for what must have been the rude words of the old hunter."[25] This authenticity that Williams found when searching through the original documents of America's past rather than the diluted versions of the history books was expressed in the term the "local"; and this concept led Creeley, as well as others, to realize that poetry must be made of words that are concrete, specific, real. Williams had said in a 1932 letter to Kay Boyle, "Art can be made of anything—provided it be seen, smelt, touched, apprehended and understood to be what it is—the flesh of a constantly repeated permanence."[26] "No ideas but in things," he said often in *Paterson*, and Creeley has repeated that phrase even more often.

Furthermore, a concern for "things" will lead the poet to realize the fact of his own self in a particular time and place and to realize the possibility of recording that fact. Creeley noted in 1961, "The LOCAL is NOT a place but a place in a given man—what part of it he has been compelled or else brought by love to give witness to in his own mind."[27] A year later in a review of *Pictures from Brueghel* he gave his understanding of *"No ideas but in things"*: "all which moves to an *elsewhere* of abstractions, of specious 'reliefs,' must be seen as false. We live as and where we are."[28] America is important to an American poet because that is where he is; it is the fact of his existence. Both Creeley and Williams, however, go beyond this to claim that the American, at least until recently, had an advantage as a poet in that the American environment was peculiarly suited to throwing fact upon the individual. "There is a persistent literalness in American writing—very much so in the tradition with which we are concerned—and it has never been easily 'symbolic.' "[29] Explaining this to an Englishman in 1964 Creeley said, "When one lives in the States, even so recently as, say, my own childhood, the terms of that environment are most usually ones that demand an immediate recognition of facts and substantial data in that environment. Now this is what Williams meant, I think, when he said, 'No ideas but in things.' It's the old characteristic that has become so associated with American pragmatism."[30]

The fact of a particular time and place has its prosodic counterpart for Williams in his use of common American speech, what he came to call "The American Idiom," which is, of course, part of the free verse experiment of this century. However, this is to simplify more than is necessary. Williams was not interested in a line without measure, but rather with substituting a different concept of measure that would both reflect the authenticity of American speech patterns and provide the requisite form upon which the fact of the poem can be built. In a 1953 letter to Richard Eberhart he said, "Whitman with his so-called free verse was wrong: there can be no absolute freedom in verse. You must have a measure but a relatively expanded measure to exclude what has to be excluded and to include what has to be included."[31] Although Creeley pointed out in a later introduction to a collection of Whitman's poems that Whitman's line is not free in the sense used here,[32] the point remains that Williams wanted a line in which the accents were free to come and go as the sense of the line demanded, and his "variable foot" was understood by Creeley, if not used in exactly the way that Williams used it.

But what happens when speech rhythms are introduced, modified in varying degrees, into the formal structure of a poem? Do the poem's rhythms simply become less formal? Is the tone of the poem simply altered? Creeley believes that more than this happens. Conversation in poetry is not the same as conversation in a conversational setting because the fact of the poem's presence changes the effect that conversation has on the listener. The poem does not just become more authentic; it also becomes more intense.[33] Creeley is apparently less interested in the fact that American speech patterns lend authenticity to the poem, a kind of immediacy of experience—although he accepts that as part of the function of common speech in poetry—and more interested in the fact that such patterns allow the poet to approximate the rhythms and patterns he hears as he creates the poem—or as the poem creates itself.[34] In a 1961 review of a collection of poems by Ed Dorn, Creeley wrote, "The *line* is, after all, the *measure* of the man writing, his term, peculiarly, as he writes, weighing, in the silence to follow, the particular word sense, necessary to his own apprehension of the melody, the tune—that he *hears*, to write."[35]

V   Olson and Zukofsky

It is at this point of emphasis that Creeley and Williams diverge and that Creeley and Charles Olson begin to share a common view of metrics that was expressed by Olson in his "Projective Verse." It is interesting to note that the first part of Olson's essay is based on letters written to Creeley during the early period of their friendship. In 1965 Creeley spoke of the extent of his debt to Olson and what it was that Olson had given him. "Olson was the first reader I had, the first man both sympathetic and articulate enough to give me a very clear sense of what the effect of my writing was, in a way that I could make use of it. . . . At the same time, his early senses of how I might make the line intimate to my own habits of speaking—that is, the groupings and whatnot that I was obviously involved with—was a great release for me."[36]

Olson's essay is at times difficult; certainly most of it is too specific to be put in other terms, but it is possible to summarize several points relevant to a discussion of Creeley's poetics and to see how Creeley's thoughts may have been crystallized by Olson's essay, keeping in mind that Creeley and Olson had already discussed these ideas. In Part I Olson defines open verse, also referred to as projective verse and composition by field, by means of an electronics analogy. Think of the poem in terms of energy rather than substance, energy spurting across from poet to reader in the moment of the poem's springing to life. ("ONE PERCEPTION MUST IMMEDIATELY AND DIRECTLY LEAD TO A FURTHER PERCEPTION.")[37] A poem seen as an energy field with the parts in active tension demands its own method of composition, its own "rules" of composition. Preconceived conventions such as meter, line length, and stanza forms are unacceptable since each poem must be formed out of its own demands and must take shape as the form evolves from the insistence of the poem as it is the process of being created. To be more concise: "FORM IS NEVER MORE

THAN AN EXTENSION OF CONTENT."[38] Olson is suggesting
then that the movement of the poem, its combination of rhythms,
sounds, images, theme, and other patterns of parts, must come from
some basic sense of appropriateness within the poet/poem as the
poem is being created/is creating itself. The poet senses this as right
just as the sympathetic reader will sense this as right when involving
himself in the poem. The reader's role is active and dynamic partici-
pation.

Olson would have been the last to claim this as original, but he
did feel a need to restate it, especially within the context of what he
feared to be a slide back to traditional versification on the part of
many American poets in the late 1940s.

This then is the principle and movement of open verse as opposed
to formal closed verse, but precisely how does it work? What should
the poet be doing in order to produce poetry based on the demands
of its own statement? In response to these questions Olson concen-
trates on two elements in the poem that must work together intimately and that give to the poem its form. The syllable—"the king
and pin of versification"—is the basic unit of the poem, smaller than
the word and therefore freer from preconceptions of usage. It can
respond on a purer, more intense level to demands on it as sound,
and it can also be arranged and rearranged endlessly, giving greater
rhythmic possibility. Superimposing the pentameter, for instance,
on this flexibility would be foolish, although the poem may well
demand a basically pentameter rhythm for its completion. Basing
form on a linguistic unit smaller than the word immediately reduces
the role that theme traditionally played in poetry and also, Olson
believed, necessitates greater intellectual discrimination on the part
of the poet because sound, the basis of the syllable, is understood by
the mind. Therefore, "The HEAD, by way of the EAR, to the
SYLLABLE."[39]

But Olson's more provocative—and more easily misunderstood—assertion involves the line: "The HEART, by way of the
BREATH, to the LINE."[40] The line breaks thus depend upon the
breathing of the poet at the moment of the poem's creation,
suggesting again the immediacy of the act of the poem and also the
link between the poem's creation and the physical context, including the poet, of that creation. In one of the most quoted passages of
the essay, he says: "And the line comes (I swear it) from the breath,
from the breathing of the man who writes, at the moment that he

writes, and thus is, it is here that, the daily work, the WORK, gets in, for only he, the man who writes, can declare, at every moment, the line its metric and its ending—where its breathing, shall come to, termination."[41]

The line, therefore, provides a relatively stable base upon which the poet can place (or the poem can demand) his combinations of syllables; and it also gives to each poem a uniqueness of form, since the context of the poem's creation will never be duplicated—the poet will never breathe exactly that way again.

Two other points must be made. First, Olson maintains that a determination of line by breath allows force and energy of speech to enter the poem, but a speech that is now transformed—energized—by its inclusion in a poetic field. Olson defined "field" as "the large area of the whole poem . . . where all the syllables and all the lines must be managed in their relations to each other."[42] The poem becomes more charged with energy, and the speech takes on added freshness. The link here with Williams' American Idiom is obvious; [43] Williams in fact printed most of the first half of the essay in his *Autobiography.*

The second point is related to the advantages that the typewriter gives to the poet, advantages primarily of precision. Even without the use of traditional meter, the poet can orchestrate his verse with precise placement of letters and punctuation, thus indicating exactly how the lines should be read. In poetry that depends upon duplicating the breath units, such control is crucial.

These then are the points of Olson's essay most closely tied to Creeley's poetry.[44] For a young poet writing in 1950 and dissatisfied with the models offered by the academics, the effect was liberating and reassuring. The natural desire to reject past conventions was given theoretical support in the sense that these conventions were imposed from outside the poem, whereas the alternative was open verse, using the energy inherent in speech by way of the syllable (sound) and giving to this speech an element of control found in the line (breath).

Creeley has written and spoken often of his own demands for poetry that is organic, but he consistently comes back to this essay as a point of departure. Writing in 1953, he discussed what he felt were the particularly useful parts of "Projective Verse." First, composition by field allows for the coherence of a poem based on the tensions among the parts with the breath as an exact, physiological

measurer of the poetic line; and, second, the use of speech allows
the poet to "find the character of his own language."[45]

A central point in understanding what Creeley finds in Olson and
therefore what he thinks happens when poetry is made is the notion
that time stands still in a poem, both in its creation by the poet and
in its re-creation by the reader or listener. The poem, both men
assert, is not something that proceeds through time from point to
point or from image to image but is rather something composed of
parts forming a whole, the whole poem being the form that the
experience-on-poet demands. The line is there as a physical unit of
measure, physical as breathing is physical and intimate as speaking
is intimate, with the rhythmic patterns of those lines (based on the
syllable) determined by the intelligence and feeling of the poet. The
poet then for Creeley works upon a "field" as defined by Olson,
rather than through sequence and consequence. Olson said that the
poem should proceed from perception to perception, but for
Creeley the poem usually consists of one perception given in a
delicate point of suspended time.

This is theory, of course. In actual practice it is impossible to
arrive at any consensus among intelligent people as to when a particular line should be broken. String any Creeley poem (or better
yet, any Olson poem) out on a line and ask each person to break that
line into as many parts as he wishes and at any point that he wishes
and the result would be a like number of poems. Which is precisely
Creeley's—and Olson's—point; each poetic field reflects intimately
the way each poet hears the syllables and lines. It is as personal as
breathing. This concept is undoubtedly linked with the care that
Creeley takes at a public reading to say the poems exactly as he feels
them, going back to begin again if the poem does not feel right for
him.

One other older contemporary is quoted repeatedly by Creeley.
Louis Zukofsky, writing quietly and steadily in New York City for
the past forty years, consistently reinforced Creeley's own notions of
what poetry should do. In a 1965 review of *ALL*, a collection of short
poems, Creeley offered a summary of Zukofsky's poetics. "Louis
Zukofsky has defined his poetics as a function, having as lower limit,
speech, and upper limit, song. It is characteristic of him to say that a
poet's ' . . . major aim is not to show himself but that order that of
itself can speak to all men. . . .' It is his belief that a poet writes one
poem all his life, a continuing *song*, so that no division of its own

existence can be thought of as being more or less than its sum. This is to say, it *all* is."[46]

In the same year he also said of Zukofsky, "I would take Zukofsky's sense of enjoying poetry with reference to the pleasure it offers as sight, sound, and intellection. These would offer for me three primary conditions of a poem's activity, and I would much respect them."[47] Zukofsky offered nothing to Creeley that had not already been offered by Pound, Williams, and Olson; but Creeley continues to find in Zukofsky's poetry standards by which others can be measured. "Louis Zukofsky's use for poets now is very great. . . . He teaches the articulation of consciousness, the modes of apprehension which words can make clear."[48]

VI *Black Mountain*

Many other poets of course share Creeley's poetic concerns or are admired by him. Creeley first came to poetry during his years at Harvard and shortly thereafter when he met such writers as Slater Brown, Kenneth Koch, and John Hawkes, and the students associated with the *Harvard Advocate* and its opposing number, *The Wake*, which published Creeley's first poems. But it was not until his move to Mallorca, where he lived from 1952 until 1955, and his contact with and subsequent living with the people at Black Mountain that Creeley began to develop some sense of where he might go with his poetry. Although Creeley and others disavow the notion of a "school," much has been written about the Black Mountain poets.[49] In an attempt to introduce British readers to the Black Mountain poets, Charles Tomlinson published a short anthology in a 1964 issue of *The Review: A Magazine of Poetry and Criticism*. The poets included in addition to Creeley were Olson, Zukofsky, Robert Duncan, Gary Snyder, Ed Dorn, Jonathan Williams, Denise Levertov, Irving Layton, Allen Ginsberg, Paul Blackburn, and Gael Turnbull. This certainly comprises a satisfactory list, although names such as Joel Oppenheimer, Fielding Dawson, Michael Rumaker, and Tom Field might be added as well as Cid Corman, since it was Corman's magazine, *Origin*, which first gave to many of these poets, including Creeley, a reliable forum. In a recent interview, Creeley was asked for the "common characteristics of the Black Mountain group." His reply: "I'd almost say—the *loner* quality each seems to have. There really isn't a common idiom, so to speak. . . . I think there was a common feeling that verse was something *given* one to write, and that the form it might then take was intimate with that fact."[50]

Creeley's role at Black Mountain College and with the *Black Mountain Review*, which he edited in its entirety from Spring 1954 to Autumn 1957,[51] is described in the final chapter of Martin Duberman's masterful history of that school, *An Exploration in Community: Black Mountain*. Here, too, diversity appears as a major characteristic of the faculty and students during the final years of the college's existence. Although it is unlikely that Creeley's poetry was affected directly by his stay at Black Mountain, the milieu of the place must have made considerable impact. The school was largely unstructured, with people coming and going constantly, courses springing up on mere whim, much of the instruction informal or tutorial, and much of the learning occurring through doing—painting, writing poetry, composing music, and so forth. In short, education took place the way it should take place, provided budgets were not there to be met. Socially, the college existed much as communes were to exist during the next decade. In fact, Duberman sees Black Mountain as prefiguring the "counterculture" that emerged in the 1960s "both in its life style of loosely related tribal council, and in a value structure that emphasized honesty in human interaction, distaste for an ethic of possession and accumulation, and the reserving of highest respect not for the abstract intellect, but for how it showed itself, was used and useful, in one's life."[52] Creeley had opposed the literary establishment before coming to Black Mountain—the *Black Mountain Review* was his conscious effort at giving publication to writers rejected by such "establishment" (i.e., new critic) reviews such as *Kenyon* and *Sewanee*—and his antiestablishment penchant could only have been strengthened during his stay at the school.

The relationship between Allen Ginsberg and the Black Mountain group illustrates the range of poetry acceptable within the group and also the difficulty of describing such a varied crew as a "school." Tomlinson apparently includes Ginsberg in his list because Ginsberg published in the *Black Mountain Review* and was listed as a contributing editor of the last issue. Shortly after the review folded due to lack of financial backing, Creeley traveled to San Francisco and there met Ginsberg, and the two have remained good friends ever since. A cursory examination of their respective poetry would suggest wide differences between them—Ginsberg's line sprawling across the page and Creeley's tight, taut line; Ginsberg's open palms and Creeley's tense fist—and yet they share many concerns, the most important being a total commitment to the serious business of poetry and the concept that "Form is never more than an extension of content." Ginsberg's line just as much as Creeley's comes from the impulse to form that Pound, Williams, and Olson helped to define. Creeley's breath unit is usually quick, short, often delicately maintained, whereas Ginsberg uses, at least since the mid-1950s, the "Hebraic-Melvillian bardic breath"; the lines differ, but the principle is the same, and Creeley certainly recognizes this. But beyond the purely technical concerns for poetry, Ginsberg gave something else to Creeley. In 1965 he said, "Allen reassured me as Williams had that my emotions were not insignificant, that their articulation was really what I was given to be involved with."[53] Different though their poetry is, Creeley and Ginsberg share much more than their friendship.

VII *Poetry, Music, and Art*

And, finally, Creeley has repeatedly indicated his debt, especially during the early years, to certain musicians, painters, and sculptors, finding a sympathetic impulse to his own work in jazz, abstract expressionist painting, and minimal sculpture. Creeley was introduced to jazz while attending Harvard, and it immediately became important to him and to his poetry. As he himself has said, "I was frankly doing almost nothing else [from 1946 to 1950] but sitting around listening to records"[54] and attending jazz sessions in and around Boston. Perhaps unknown to him then but certainly clear in hindsight, these musicians were doing things with music that he was struggling to do with words. Miles Davis, Thelonious Monk, and especially Charlie Parker demonstrated that feelings could be expressed freely and directly, with no apology and no necessity to place those feelings within a prescribed form or pattern. The individual work would pursue its own demands. This notion corresponds closely to the ideas of Williams and particularly Olson in "Projective Verse," but the contact for Creeley was made in music several years before it was made in poetry. Those years during the war and immediately following were years, as Creeley has said, of chaos on the one hand and of the demands for traditional restrictions on the other, restrictions of life and restrictions of art. Jazz demonstrated that the individual could go beyond compartmentaliza-

tion of intellect and feeling to "an intensive and an absolutely full
experience of whatever it was you were engaged with."[55] His contact
with jazz was at least as liberating in its way as his later contact with
Olson and Ginsberg would prove to be.

But jazz was liberating also in a more specifically poetic sense.
Creeley has commented often of the influence of jazzmen on the
early development of his poetry, particularly as they demonstrated
how measure can be loosened and varied, freeing the musician—
and the poet—from regular, controlled, preordained pattern.
"Line-wise, the most complementary sense I have found is that of
musicians like Charlie Parker and Miles Davis. I am interested in
how that is done, how 'time' there is held to a measure peculiarly an
evidence (a hand) of the emotion which prompts (drives) the poem
in the first place."[56] For the jazz musician—as for Creeley—the line
comes out of the experience of the moment through a combination
of intelligence and feeling. And that line vibrates not to a preconceived pattern but to the demands of the music itself. Charlie
Parker's use of time fascinated Creeley: how a jazz piece could
conflate or stretch a moment and could make infinitely more variable the rhythmic alternatives in a line. Creeley saw in this music
the primacy of sound. As he said later, a poem depends on the way it
is presented and not on its subject. So too with jazz. The substantiality, the reality of the work created is in the work itself and not in
some abstraction it inclines toward. Jazz was where Creeley was
hearing " 'things said' in terms of rhythmic and sound possibilities."[57]

And to a large extent he was seeing these possibilities in the
paintings and painters he also came to know, particularly in the
early 1950s. He had met René Laubiés, a translater of Pound as well
as a painter, while in Europe; in fact, Laubiés drew the cover for
Creeley's second book of poems. *The Kind of Act Of,* and contrib-
uted drawings to his third book, *The Immoral Proposition* (1953);
and he had met other painters while living in Mallorca. Black Mountain, however, provided his most consistent contact with painters
including, among others, Jackson Pollock, whom Creeley had met
earlier and whose paintings he had first seen in a Paris gallery;
Ashley Bryan, who did the cover for his first volume, *Le Fou;* John
Altoon, whose importance to Creeley is described briefly in *A Day
Book;* Franz Kline, whose statement, "Painting is paint," is quoted

often; John Chamberlain, a sculptor and friend; as well as Guston, deKooning, Vincente, and Motherwell.[58]

Most of these painters were working within the context of abstract expressionism, which meant for Creeley that they too were concerned with the work of art as an entity rather than with what it could represent. Words are the material of poetry; paint is the material of painting; and even more specifically, the contact between painters such as Pollock and Creeley is in their common view that the work is where the action takes place. Creeley often quotes Pollock's statement: "When I am in my painting, I am not aware of what I am doing," and in a 1963 interview with the British poet Charles Tomlinson, he continued that quotation: "I have no fears about making changes or destroying images because the painting has a life of its own."[59] So too does the poem for Creeley. In fact, perhaps the statement concerning poetry that is closest to the position of the abstract expressionists is Olson's "Projective Verse," that seminal work that so much involved Creeley. And, finally, Creeley saw in the work of these painters and sculptors that acknowledgment of the self-contained reality of the physical object ("No ideas but in things") that has been his constant realization throughout the years. Speaking of these artists, he said in 1967, "We were making things in the materials particular to our own experience of things, just as John Chamberlain was experiencing the particular fact of materials in his world, e.g. those car parts, and seeing how the imagination might articulate that experience; I was trying to make do with the vocabulary in terms of experience in my world."[60] Here as in jazz, Creeley recognized the unique utterance and freedom from external or preconceived notions and forms that he was in the process of discovering for his own poetry and fiction.

Poets, musicians, painters, and sculptors, dissimilar in many ways, can give much to each other, and these particular symbiotic relationships are just several of the many Creeley has managed to maintain over the years. Although he confesses to being a loner and has often searched out remote places in which to work, nevertheless, Creeley is presently at the center of a vital, exciting creative scene composed of friends, fellow poets, artists, teachers, former students, aspiring poets, and varying degrees of cult followers who keep the important issues of poetry seething but who also make exhausting demands on Creeley—as he on them. Surely one of the most impressive energy centers in our society must be a poetry conference attended by Creeley.

From the first tentative letters to Pound and Williams, through discussions in southern France with Denise Levertov, contact with Olson, the editing of *Black Mountain Review* and subsequent teaching at the college, meetings with Ginsberg and the San Francisco poets, and the growing recognition of his own poetry, Creeley has gradually assumed an important place in contemporary American poetry, even to the point where younger poets are writing what an interviewer in the *Paris Review* called "Creeley poems—short, terse, poignant."[61] And it must be remembered that he is only at the midpoint of his career.

CHAPTER 2

Pieces

THE simple fact is that with *Pieces* in 1969, Robert Creeley's poetry shuddered onto another level of intensity. As a fire being shaken down to make the coals burn brighter (though he rejected "the damn function of *simile*, always a displacement of what *is* happening"[1] and said elsewhere, "I hate the metaphors" [76]), so his poetry was shaken until the words alone remained, not as referents for objects but as objects. The shift is this:

> You want
> the fact
> of things
> in words,
> of words. (61)

This is the simple fact: the reality and sufficiency of the word, the word become thing. Two years earlier he had published a volume called *Words;* five years later he was to publish a slim volume called *Thirty Things.* Of course. This has been the direction of his poetry over the past fifteen years, a direction made clear and emphatic with the publication of *Pieces.* Louis Martz, writing in the *Yale Review,* sensed the success of Creeley's effort: "It is impossible, I believe, to become more abstract without destroying the very presence of poetry. Yet Creeley manages to hold himself at the taut edge of poetic existence."[2] And Creeley's friend, Denise Levertov, answering possible charges of vagueness or carelessness, responded, "In *Pieces* something different happens—or *is* happening, for it is anything but a static work. . . . Its very sprawl and openness, its notebook quality, its absence of perfectionism, Creeley letting his hair down, is in fact a movement of energy in his work, to my ear, not a breaking down but a breaking open."[3] The volume caused considerable controversy; not everyone agreed with Martz

and Levertov. In fact, several reviewers saw it as a retreat for
Creeley. Charles Potts, in an article entitled, *"Pieces:* The Decline
of Robert Creeley," said: *"Pieces* is nothing if not narrower in range
than Creeley's earlier work."[4] Other reviewers were even more
blunt in their criticism. Daniel Hughes, in a brief note in the *Massachusetts Review,* said: "Robert Creeley's poems, especially in
Pieces, are all theory and not a very interesting one at that";[5] and
Reed Whittemore, writing in *The New Republic,* called *Pieces* a
preaching book disguised behind an antipreaching pose, leaving
him with "a sense of emotional and experiential emptiness."[6] Even
the negative reviews, however, responded to the increasing lean-
ness of Creeley's already taut, spare, minimal style, reflecting his
increasing obsession with going beyond things to words and beyond
the referents of those words to the words as objects, as pieces.

I   *The Word Become Thing*

The following poem begins with Creeley pasting words on the
page:

> One/ the Sun/
> Moon/ one.

and then moves to as overt a statement as Creeley makes concerning
his desire that the word become thing.

> The pen,
> the lines it
> leaves, forms
> divine—nor
> laugh nor giggle.
> This prescription
> is true.
> Truth is a scrawl,
> all told
> in all. (36)

The insistence in this section that the pen is a teller of truth borders
on the cliché, but Creeley is actually reinvesting this idea with some
of its original impact by focusing on the literal lines left by the
moving pen and by concluding his poem with the simple insistence,

>Words
>are
>pleasure.
>All
>words. (37)

Most often, however, Creeley uses the insistence of words as facts to
substantiate the poem rather than discussing it overtly as in the
above examples. The result is the simple tautness of many of the
poems in *Pieces* as words are tapped into the pattern of the volume.
One poem begins:

>One thing
>done, the
>rest follows. (13)

These lines, demonstrating how easily commentary can become inadequate when placed beside the spare statement that is the poem,
express the organic concept in poetry, perhaps in life. At any rate,
an event produces its inevitable consequence. But that commentary
is already too abstract, too corroded. Look again at this section.
"Done" is placed on a separate line, and as the eye and voice pause
and then drop down one line, the finality of the act is emphasized,
gently. The consequence is begun on the same line and then drops
down one more line to remain complete on that line. But, even the
cursory reader might insist that all this is quite obvious. Precisely,
but the presence of those words on that page is what is real, and that
is too easily overlooked. The poem ends with even simpler insistence:

>Here here
>here. Here. (14)

The reader might again object that anyone could put four "heres" on
a page, but Creeley has done this within the context of the poem,
squaring them, to give the visual, almost kinesthetic sense of solidity and stability found in the fourth poem of the sequence, "Numbers," also found in *Pieces*. One might further argue that placing a
period between the last two "heres" gives more physical presence to
this line, allowing the first line to rest more easily on it; and, finally,

a period allows the final "here" to be capitalized thus providing a diagonal balance for the section. This may be saying too much about four "heres"; however, the fact of those four words inlaid into the poem needs to be noted.

In still another poem, Creeley uses delicately simple words and syntax to suggest both physical presence and physical movement. "3 In 1" is in one sense less abstract than many other poems in this volume because it rests upon an outside observable phenomenon, the flight of a bird; but in another sense—and a sense crucial to an awareness of what Creeley is attempting in these poems—this poem is more abstract because the presence of an outside phenomenon makes ultimately impossible the sufficiency of those words in that poem. The referents are there; however, the poem rides on its own physical insistence.

> The bird
> flies
> out the
> window. She
> flies.
>
> The bird flies
> out the
> window. She
> flies.
>
> The bird
> flies. She
> flies. (46–47)

The poem consists of an image presented as economically as possible in three different versions. A physical feature of the first section is the repetition of the idea in two words with the first word "She" placed on the same line with the conclusion of the image, the effect being a sudden movement, suggesting, of course, the moment of the bird's flight. Simple, but then this physical movement is repeated, again gently and delicately, in the two following sections, where the movement is quickened and then released. This is difficult poetry because the fragility produces a very small margin for error. Here is not the secure haze between two halves of a metaphor.

II *The Captured Moment*

But this is only part of Creeley's design. In order to heighten the reality of the word, Creeley in this volume attempts what he admits to be impossible—to isolate the moment. Even while the individual flows through time, he must attempt somehow to wrench a moment out of that flux and hold it to the page. Mystics claim success at this; Creeley never does, although he never stops trying; and it is this two way pull of attempt and failure that produces the desperately clutching tone of many of the poems in *Pieces*. The word can literally become flesh only if torn from the living flesh of time, and this is torturous activity. Fragments, pieces, grunts, gasps, but also nudgings and cajolings. The reality and sufficiency of the word within the almost captured, fleeting moment, this is Creeley's method in *Pieces*, and it has produced poems of flash point brevity and intensity.

Creeley's creeping up on the moment to a final, simple insistence can be seen in his poem, " 'Time' is some sort of hindsight," which moves from definition and example to assertion.

"Time" is some sort of hindsight, or else rhythm of activity
—e.g., now it's 11 days later—"also alive" like they say.
        .
Where it is
was and
will be never
only here.
        .
—fluttering as
  falling, leaves,
  knives, to
  avoid—tunnel
  down the
  vague sides . . .
        .
—it
  it— (17)

Following a somewhat prosaic and tentative definition, Creeley in section two manipulates tense in an intentionally blunted attempt to suggest the "only here" of the section's final line. Section three moves beyond this, however, to the subtle precariousness of the image. The opposites of past and future—"was" and "will be"—are echoed in the equally opposing movement of fluttering, birdlike ascension and of falling; of the tactile as well as connotative differences between leaves and knives that are held in attraction by their visual similarity; and of tunnel with its hard definiteness and its vague sides, reflecting the sharp but irregular paths of the falling leaves. All are distinct opposites but each pair suggests an unidentifiable point precisely between the opposing extremes. The poem then moves to the final section in which the attempt to locate is abandoned and the pronoun is captured between two dashes, themselves transitional devices when used in normal contexts but here holding up the two "its" like bookends. This movement from inadequate definition to assertion is the movement from the complex to the simple, from the abstract to the concrete, passing through a series of unsuccessful attempts, producing a faltering hesitancy when the third unsuccessful attempt is left incomplete, and then reconciling itself in the final, almost timid but perhaps just properly modest assertion.

Even in more complex poems Creeley attempts to capture the moment or perhaps a series of moments in a variety of ways. The following poem alternates between a syntactical attempt at trapping the reality of the moment between words or phrases and an insistence on that moment through the insistent stamping of words into the poem.

Having to—
what do I think
to say now.

Nothing but
comes and goes
in a moment

Cup.
Bowl.
Saucer.
Full.

The way into the form
the way out of the room—

The door, the hat,
the chair, the fact.

> Sitting, waves on the beach,
> or else clouds, in the sky,
> a road, going by,
> cars, a truck, animals, in crowds. (6–7)

The poem begins with a pause, a momentary but unclear stop, "Having to—." And what is put into that vacuum? The answer is whatever is there at the moment, and Creeley itemizes, with the emphasis on "item," the noun: vertically as in section two, horizontally as in the final line, and in his favorite, stable square as in the second half of the third section. The vertical-horizontal shapes are not alone in giving form to this poem. Unobtrusive rhyme and near rhyme bind the items loosely together: Bowl/ Full, form/ room, hat/ fact, sky/ by, and the internal clouds/ crowds of the final four lines. Sections two, three, and four can be seen as appositives to "Nothing but/ comes and goes/ in a moment," and this answers the question, "What do I think to say now," which, in turn, fills in the moment's pause following "Having to—." Time stops, in a sense, while the poem attempts to define that moment in terms of form (cup, bowl, door, hat) and movement (comes and goes, into, out of, sitting, going).

The use of form and motion to suggest a moment in time demands, as seen in the preceding poems, either a simple directness or a shifting elliptical pattern; that is, the poet either meets the moment head on, pretending in a sense that he is unaware of the impossibility of his task, or he must come at that moment from an angle or even from many angles. At any rate, the resulting poem is likely to be arranged nonsequentially. The following poem, "Place," must be seen neither as a rational construct (cause and effect) nor as an imagistic pattern (one image suggesting the next) but rather as a tightening or screwing up of the string to a higher and higher pitch. The lines become progressively less syntactically normal, and the jump from section to section less rational.

> Thinking of you asleep on a
> bed on a pillow, on a
> bed—the ground or space
>
> you lie on. That's enough to
> talk to now I got space and
> time like a broken watch

Hello there—instant
reality on the other
end of this so-called line.

Oh no you
don't, do you?

Late, the words, late
the form of them, al-

ready past what they were
fit for, one and two and three. (43)

As the title suggests, "Place" is a point in space as well as a point in
time, and, again, the attempt is made to hold it. Ironies abound. In
section one the space that a person occupies is real, but is it? The
speaker after all has only the thought of it. That seems to be
sufficient, but is it? The broken watch is its symbol; time is made to
stand still, but artificially and through destruction. Even the use of
one of Creeley's rare similes ("like a broken watch") makes us suspect the sincerity of the comparison. The jump to the next section is
produced by the link between "talk to" and the telephone conversation of section two. The ironic absurdity of talking to reality on a
"so-called line" is apparent enough, but the jump to the next section
is not. Is this a trivial part of the telephone conversation? Perhaps,
but it is also a moment between conclusions. "Oh no you/ don't, do
you?" suggests that what follows will be an unwanted answer, and so
the inevitable reply is forever suspended, but, and here we move to
the final section, forever suspended in words, the words of this
poem. The words, he says, are "al-/ ready past what they were fit
for," but the poem remains as a permanent thing, while time whirls
past it. The final irony then is Creeley's claim that he cannot do what
he has just done: capture the moment.

In many of these poems Creeley struggles (the success is *in* the
struggle) for the moment, surrounding it, jabbing and flicking, allowing syntax to crumble in a controlled disintegration, energy
using itself up. In one poem a place is suggested,

In the house of
old friend, whose
friend, my

friend, the trouble

> with you, who,
> he is, there, here,
> we were *not*.

ending with the simple statement,

> we are
> all around what we are. (55)

Or elsewhere, time is surrounded by tense:

> What have I seen,
> now see? There were
> times before
> I look now. (59)

And in still another poem Creeley goes from absolute certainty to absolute uncertainty, from platitude to humility in four lines:

> Each moment constitutes reality,
> or rather may constitute
> reality, or may have *done*
> so, or perhaps *will*? (62)

Even in the occasional longer poem, Creeley is able to suggest the importance of the moment either because the long poem is a collection of moments or because he insists and insists again on the unique physical existence of the word. "Numbers" is a poem sequence on the numbers one through nine to zero in which Creeley probes the significance of these numbers, exploring in a tentative way their various meanings and uses through history and their more immediate and personal meaning for him. But the impact of the numbers depends upon their physical presences in the poems as words. Their shapes, their weight, their literal relationships are continually underscored. "One" begins: "What / singular upright flourishing/ condition . . ." and ends:

> As of a stick,
> stone, some-
>
> thing so
> fixed it has
>
> a head, walks,
> talks, leads
>
> a life. (21–22)

"Six" begins: "Twisting," and ends: "Or two triangles interlocked"
(27–28). "Eight": "Say 'eight'—" ending with:

> Oct-
> ag-
> on-
> al. (29–31)

Each number is examined as by a man with a stick in a darkened
cellar, so that the physical presence is not all that is discovered but it
is what is most immediately known. Here is the number "Four":

> This number for me
> is comfort, a secure
> fact of things. The
>
> table stands on
> all fours. The dog
> walks comfortably,
>
> and two by two
> is not an army
> but friends who love
>
> one another. Four
> is a square,
> or peaceful circle,
>
> celebrating return,
> reunion,
> love's triumph.
>
> The card which is the
> four of hearts must
> mean enduring experience
> of life. What other
> meaning could it have.
>
> Is a door
> four—but
> who enters.
>
> Abstract—yes, as
> two and two
> things, four things—
> one and three. (25–26)

The solidity and stability of the number four is most obvious with its four corners. Comfort, security, yes, but beyond that a precise kind of love—not the love of lovers (that was described in "Two," following the phallic "One," and followed by the "first triangle . . . a lonely occasion"), but the love of four people for each other. Any more would be a mob or an army. Transfer this stability to an abstraction such as the significance of the four of hearts and the result is "enduring experience of life." The final section of "Four" overtly rejects the notion of four as an abstraction. It is "two and two/ things, four things—/ one and three." But always things.

It is tempting perhaps to dismiss "Numbers" as a gimmick, a simple stringing together of separate poems linked only by the convenience of a number sequence. But this poem, called by Louis Martz "the finest sequence in the book,"[7] does present a continuing, growing concern for a person's life, which carries from number to number, beginning with the male-female relationship of the first numbers ("Six" includes: "contains/ the first even number/ (2), and the first odd/ number (3), the former representing/ the male member, and the latter/ the *muliebris pudenda* . . .' "), continuing through a growing sense of responsibility (Wordsworth's "We Are Seven"), through the realization of time's passing in "Eight" ("Now summer fades./ August its month—"), through the breakup of certainties in "Nine" ("There is no point/ of rest here./ It wavers"), to the final paradox of "Zero" ("Where are you—who/ by not being here/ are here, but here/ by not being here?"), and finally, to the coda titled "The Fool." All work into the pattern, but the substantiality of the poem rests upon the fact of the numbers themselves.

III   *The Pattern of* Pieces: *Poem as Journal*

This then is Creeley's method in *Pieces*. Most if not all of the poems in this volume hover precariously on the edge of self-sufficiency, momentarily outside time, not really needing any external frames of reference; they are, even as the words are, their own reality. They are, in fact, pieces. At this point, however, another characteristic of this volume asserts itself. Paradoxically, these separate poems that seem so self-sufficient tend to organize themselves in the minds of readers into interrelated patterns. Not neatly necessarily, but perceptibly. Russell Banks argues in *Lillabulero* that *Pieces* "reads like a single, book-length poem," moving sequentially

from "the assertion of particularity" through a "depth of anxiety" to a
final joyful turning to other people.[8] Although Banks may be too
insistent on the specific pattern of the book, he does demonstrate
convincingly that the volume has an interrelatedness that can be
easily overlooked. Denise Levertov is more accurate when she
claims less for the book's organization: "they [the poems] are all
related, it's a complete book, the way a notebook or diary has its
own completedness and coherence, a relatedness of part to part that
is not identical with the coherence of the deliberately arranged. . . ."[9] This view of *Pieces* as a kind of working poet's journal, understood more easily in light of Creeley's subsequent long
prose work called *A Day Book* in which he is doing something of the
same thing, reveals the loose structure of the volume as a series of
common concerns and strategies.

As is true of most journal writers, Creeley continually returns to
certain considerations in this volume, providing a structural thread
as well as rhythmic pattern to these seemingly random fragments.
Two such concerns, search for perception of self and search for
perception of form, flicker through these poems as pinpoints of
delicate balance, hovering momentarily before disappearing into
the next attempt. Perception of self and perception of form are
untimately impossible in Creeley's poetry, of course, as seen in the
earlier unsuccessful attempts to make the word serve as an objective
reality, a thing in itself; however—and this is most crucial—again
the success of the poetry depends upon the *attempt*, the *search* for a
perception of self and form and not the attainment of some Platonic
absolute. The question then asked in many of these poems is not,
"What is the complete self and absolute form?" but rather, "How
can this self—or even fragments of it—be perceived and how can
this form be perceived?" In other words, *Pieces* deals with epis-
temology rather than metaphor, and the struggle for perception, the
tension between necessary attempt and inevitable failure, is the
landscape of Creeley's poems, a miniaturized and internalized battle
ground.

The first concern found frequently in *Pieces* is the search for
perception of self, a concern of poems discussed earlier in this chapter; however, the questions raised are more subtle than has so far
been suggested: not "Who am I?" but "What portions of me, my
present, and my past are perceivable, to what degree are they perceivable, and why are they not more completely perceivable?" It

should be understood that these two concerns—search for a perception of self and search for a perception of form—are integrally related (the self is just another form that can never be totally realized),
although, in another sense, this search for self makes even more
vital the intensely personal act of perception; it seems to place the
stakes higher.

Because the poems in *Pieces* are concerned so precisely with
delineating the interior landscape, questions of self are inevitable,
just as the immediacy of that landscape's depiction results in the
effort to make words into realities rather than surrogates for reality.
The attempt at perception of self runs through all the poems; however, in some it comes closer to the surface than in others. "Here"
begins with the knowledge that the past is not enough to explain the
present:

> Past time—those
> memories opened
> places and minds,
> things of such reassurance—
>
> now the twist,
> and what was a road
> turns to a circle
> with nothing behind.

moves to the inadequacy of all abstraction, reflecting an existential
faith in activity: "I have never known it/ but in doing found it/ as best
I could"; and then restates in the final two sections a simple faith in
the importance of the moment. The movement is inward from
"they" to "my."

> They all walk by
> on the beach,
> large, or little,
> crippled, on the face
> of the earth.
>
> The wind holds
> my leg like
>
> a warm hand. (72)

The self is discovered, at least partly, in doing and not in thinking,
although thinking may be part of the doing.

The location of self is as delicate and shifting as the fixing of a word. Both waver, dissolve, reappear, and dissolve again.

> I cannot see you
> There for what you
> thought you were.
>
> . . . .
>
> Here I
> am. There
> you are. (14)

These lines examine the paradox between the physical reality of experience and the elusive nature of the experience in time. The present is all we have, and yet we never really have it. All is incomplete, continuing, fragmentary. Creeley had said in the preface to his previous collection, *Words*: "Things continue, but my sense is that I have, at best, simply taken place with that fact. I see no progress in time or any other situation. So it is that what I feel, in the world, is one thing I know myself to be, for that instant. I will never know myself otherwise."[10]

The fragmentary nature of this perception is captured in the form as well as the theme of "ECHO OF."

> Can't myself
> let off this
> *fiction*. "You
> don't exist,
>
> baby, you're
> dead." Walk
> off, on—the
> light bulb
>
> overhead, beside,
> or, the bed, you
> think you laid
> on? When, what. (52–53)

The effect is one of incomplete rather than unanswered questions as the syntax rapidly dissolves. The dismissal of "walk off" is reversed, "on," which suggests a light bulb (off-on) over or beside a bed you lay-laid on, followed by two open-ended questions/statements. More than the difficulty is communicated here. Anguish may not be too strong a word.

In addition to providing a thread or pattern to the book, this search for perception of self at times links together, even more strongly, certain groups of poems, a practice strengthened by Creeley's unique but consistent punctuation system. The single, centered period divides separate stanzas, and the triple, centered periods divide separate poems, a practice that is particularly useful because some poems are titled and others are not.[11] In addition to this, Creeley occasionally separates poems with a single, centered period when the following poem is titled. Although all of this seems more complicated than it really is, such divisions are useful because they allow Creeley to use subtler gradations of thought divisions and relationships instead of just the usual end of stanza and end of poem, thus providing for groupings of poems within the volume but without intrusive subtopic sections.

Altogether, nine such groupings exist, with the fourth being by far the largest. The titles of the seven poems in this fourth group, all in upper case, provide an instant commentary on the location and perception of self: DICTION, AMERICA, CITIZEN, PLACE, THE PURITAN ETHOS, THE PROVINCE, and CANADA. "PLACE" is significantly the central poem, although a new pattern emerges if "DICTION" is seen as a prologuelike discussion of language in relation to the world it occupies.

> The grand time when the words
> were fit for human allegation,
>
> and imagination of small, local
> containments, and the lids fit.
>
> What was the wind blew through it,
> a veritable bonfire like they say—
>
> and did say in hostile, little voices:
> "It's changed, it's not the same!" (41)

No more do words serve the functions ascribed to them—the lids no longer fit—and those voices that lament such a loss are dismissed, guilty by association with cliché. Hostility to change in language as in life is a sign of smallness.

The new pattern puts "AMERICA" and "CANADA" at opposite ends, with "CITIZEN" and "THE PURITAN ETHOS" (political and moral anchors) at the center. "PLACE" has been discussed earlier in this chapter and can be seen, together with "THE PURITAN ETHOS," to reflect the problem of location of self in time and space. The other poems fit in through rejection of those values that destroy any useful relationship between the individual and society. "AMERICA" and "CITIZEN" are diatribes against the United States of the late 1960s, and "THE PROVINCE" and "CANADA" comment on Canadian weaknesses. The point here is that Creeley has provided a pattern within a pattern by grouping poems within the larger themes of the book.

The dichotomy between the self and the imperfect perception of that self is seen also in one of the most frequently recurring words in *Pieces*—and, indeed, in much that Creeley has written: "form." In every case this word is used as a noun rather than a verb, thus emphasizing the static rather than the evolving aspect of that word and the concept it represents. Although form is not used in precisely identical ways, it does in most cases suggest those realities that one perceives imperfectly, but that can be perceived more accurately either through more sharpened perception or through more skilled rendering of perception through words. Sharper perception is within the possibility of all people; skillful rendering of perception is the function of the poet. Neither complete perception nor perfect rendering is possible; success once again results from the attempt, and Creeley's poetry, especially in *Pieces*, reflects the breathless intensity of that struggle.

The opening poem of *Pieces* stands as a statement of form as something unattainable but necessary. In fact, while an awareness that the form is off in the future somewhere gives direction to one's efforts, the important fact remains that attainment of that form is undesirable even if possible because, again, the struggle exceeds the form itself. In that special sense, the form is inferior to the efforts at duplicating it. The poem begins: "As real as thinking/ wonders created/ by the possibility—/ forms," but quickly moves to the statement: "No forms less/ than activity." The effort and not the attainment is preferred in these lines that suggest Williams' famous dictum, "No Ideas but in Things." And still later present physical facts are enumerated:

       Small facts
       of eyes, hair
       blonde, face

       looking like a
       flat painted
       board.

The movement in the poem is from forms as possibilities to forms as active creations in physical facts to an attempt at defining the "impossible/ locations" of forms:

       reaching in
       from out-

       side, out
       from in—

       side—as
       middle:

       one
       hand. (3–4)

This poem takes on added significance when seen as the opening poem in the volume because each poem, each "piece," is a "small fact" dropped carefully into "impossible locations." In a very real sense, these poems are like the daubs of pure color in a pointillist painting, daubs mixed in the eye of the beholder.

Each Creeley poem then remains a fragment, an incomplete, partial perception, a fact often emphasized by ellipses and nonsyntactical juxtapositions of Creeley's most inaccessible poetry. The following poem is an attempt to suggest the "form/ seen" of the first section.

     The which it
     was, form
     seen—there
     here,re-
     peated for/
     as/—There
     is a "parallel."

When and/or if, as,—however, you do "speak" to people, i.e., as condition of the circumstance (as Latin: "what's

around") a/n "im(in)pression." "I'll *crush* you to death—
"flying home."

Allen last night—context of *how* include the output of of human function in an experience thereof makes the fact of it
become possibility of pleasure—not fear, not pain. Every-
body *spends* it (the "life" they inhabit) all—hence, no problem of that kind, except (*large* fact) in imagination. (54–55)

The "point" of this poem, especially in the first two sections, is the
very form it takes, and this is not meant in the usual organic
sense—form and content match—but rather in McLuhan's sense
(Creeley would object)—that the form is the content. Here, even
more obviously than in his other poetry, the words must be seen on
the page and heard as Creeley intends them to be heard, hurried,
stumbling, insistent. Section two begins with probing, changing
adverbs and ends with a terse finality, "flying home." In between is
a brief collection of wordplay and juxtapositions. Is he referring to a
type of speaking to people while "standing around" (Latin circumstance)? Does the final "in" inserted after "im" of "impression"
reinforce the physical force of "impression"? Is the stronger impression then extended to its logical conclusion in " 'I'll *crush* you to
death' "? And, finally, is a connection suggested between "death"
and "flying home"? Although the answer to all these questions is
undoubtedly yes, that is to miss the main point, which is the
impression of partial perception. The third section, a journallike
account of a conversation with another poet, puts on an abstract
level (except that it is in fact a conversation with another poet) the
problem of human perception through poetry, specifically making
all experience pleasurable through its transference into poetry.

And, finally, in a long poem near the end of *Pieces*, Creeley
attempts once more to suggest the distance between form and the
imperfect perception of it. He says, "The forms shift/ before we
know,/ before we thought/ to know it." The result of that awareness
in this poem, however, is not the excitement of struggle found
elsewhere but rather a listlessness referred to in the poem's opening
line and reflected both in the images and rhythms of much of the
poem: rising heat, vacancy, sluggishness, a lowering sun,

                         Washed
                    out—the afternoon

> of another day
> with other people,
> looking out of other eyes.

Halfway through the poem, a temporary reprieve from lethargy occurs;

> Only the
> children, the sea,
> the slight wind move
>
> with the
> same insistent
> particularity, (76–78)

but the poem returns to greyness. Unusual for Creeley in its near resignation, this poem has little of the zest for battle that characterizes many of his struggles for perception; but it is typical in its insistence that the forms can not—and should not—be completely caught.

The act of perceiving forms, especially the self, through words that are themselves physical, self-sufficient facts in moments torn from time—this is what Creeley attempts in *Pieces*. And he fails, of course. He cannot attain the form; his words remain to some extent words; and time moves relentlessly. But he tries desperately, and paradoxically, in the failed attempt he succeeds. These poems are a record of that attempt, journallike, incomplete, fragmentary. Looking back in 1974 to the composition of these poems, Creeley said that he had grown bored with the notion of poems as tidy single pieces of paper. Life continues, why not poems? Each poem then, a fact in itself, is also part of the cumulative life of the poet, working together all things, "the casual, the commonplace, that which collected itself."[12]

Perhaps, then, it is best to think of *Pieces*, finally, as pieces, pieces of a broken mirror scattered randomly. One can look into the pieces and see parts and corners of his own face; he can even begin to fill in the empty spaces, producing something recognizable; but he has always thrust upon him the awareness that the image is incomplete, fragmentary, jagged. Inadequate though it is, the broken mirror is all he has, and he must continue to look into it.

CHAPTER 3

Words

To repeat: "It is the way a poem speaks, not the matter, that proves its effects."[1] A platitude certainly in postmodern esthetics. How else does a Braque or a Franz Kline painting speak to us but through the form it takes, the "way"? The planes, the textures, the colors, these and not the matter speak to us. The way a poem then speaks, the statement it makes, is through its form. By Creeley's own insistence, this speaking succeeds through what Olson points out is basic to poetry: the syllable and the line. Syntax and sound are established by manipulating the syllable, and the poem is given physical substantiality through the line, a line determined literally by the breathing of the poet. Furthermore, for Creeley the poem is given even more substantial form by the inclusion of specific American speech patterns, patterns that Creeley insists do exist and that he identifies most strongly with William Carlos Williams' "local."

I Rhythmic Precision

What we have seen in Chapter 2 and what we now see in Creeley's 1967 collection, *Words*, is a basic concern with rhythmic precision, with matching the rhythms of each poem to the impulses of that poem and thus in effect causing the rhythmic pattern to become the vehicle through which the poem speaks. In *Pieces* Creeley literally caused the rhythm to carry the statement; in *Words* the rhythm most often works concurrently with a discernible image. An examination of several poems written in the early 1960s will illustrate both the organic matching of rhythm, image, and statement, and the range and variety of rhythmic possibilities.

WATER

The sun's
sky in
form of
blue sky
that

water will
never make
even
in
reflection.

Sing, song,
mind's form
feeling
if
mistaken,

shaken,
broken water's
forms, love's
error
in water.[2]

The first two stanzas constitute a syntactically easy sentence: a reflection of the sky in water is inferior to a direct perception of that sky; however, the sentence itself is slightly elliptical—The sun's sky in (the) form of (a) blue sky—and even incomplete; and the short lines produce a broken, jagged effect. The second half of the poem extends this perception of a physical phenomenon to its human parallel, the incapacity of a person's feelings, love perhaps, to respond sufficiently to the cause of that feeling; and, once again, the form is broken, now even more elliptical, more insistently fragmented. The perception revealed can best be understood by comparing the poem to a high speed photograph of gently agitated water with each facet of a wave, diamondlike, reflecting only a portion of the sky. The parallel to the inadequacy of human feelings then becomes clear—and hangs there suspended in time. Rhythmically, each brief line, even each syllable, underscores the fragmentary quality of the reflection and the perception, especially when each line is heavily punctuated by Creeley's reading. But the handling of syllables is subtler than that. In stanza one "Sun's/ sky" and "blue sky" reflect each other rhythmically except for the juncture in the former. No such parallel occurs in the second stanza, which asserts water's inadequacy in reflection. The shift to human feeling is made in the first line of stanza three, "Sing, song," a shift from one realm to another, the form echoing the earlier sound parallels ("Sun's/ sky" and "blue sky") and anticipating the next line, "mind's form." But then these parallel double accentual units disappear in the insistence of single accents: "mistáken," "sháken," "bróken," reflecting the fragmentary quality of these human feelings before the final easing into "love's/ error/ in water." This is not to insist that such choices were conscious on the part of the poet; rather, the choices were likely made in the act of creation.

Another poem that matches form and content, "Quick-Step," suggests rhythmically the easy grace of the dance.

> More gaily, dance
> with such ladies make
> a circumstance of dancing.
>
> Let them lead
> around and around, all
> awkwardness apart.
>
> There is
> an easy grace gained
> from falling forward
>
> in time, in
> simple time to
> all their graces. (41)

Here the lines are lengthened primarily by using more unaccented syllables and by using devices such as assonance ("all/ awkwardness apart"), alliteration ("grace gained," "falling forward,"), and internal rhyme ("circumstance of dancing"), that aid the smooth movement of the line. These are traditional poetic devices, of course, and they promote a correspondence between the poem's form and the concept of the dance, the fluid shifts in the tempo of the quick dance reflected, for instance, in the hesitation at the end of stanza three ("from falling forward") and the effortless recovery at the beginning of stanza four ("in time, in/ simple time"). Furthermore, the poem is not a poem about dancing or even about the movements of a particular dance, but rather the poem itself, the sounds, the rhythms, is a dance.

The third poem, "Song," produces still another rhythmic variation.

> The grit
> of things,
> a measure
> resistant—
>
> times walk-
> ing, talk-
> ing, telling
> lies and
>
> all the other
> places, no
> one ever
> quite the same. (28)

Here the lines are once again short, and, once again, the poem is "about" the rhythm it produces. The precision of the poem does not come from the image—"The grit/ of things" is as specific as the poem's image becomes. Rather it results from the precise rhythmic rendering of the idea of grit, namely , a grinding hesitancy resulting from the introduction of a foreign substance, as sand, into machinery. In terms of the poem's rhythm this would be "a measure/ resistant—"; in terms of human contact it would be "telling/ lies." The hesitant rhythm is introduced then in stanza two between these two corresponding ideas, the counterrhythm resulting from the simple division of words: "Walk-/ ing, talk-/ ing." The voice must pause unnaturally at those line breaks, whereas before and after, the lines proceed smoothly with syntactically acceptable breaks (although more so in the first stanza than in the third). The temptation when reading a poem such as this is to search beyond it for application. Does the poem suggest the counterproductivity of lying? Is it supporting rhythmically subtle poetry as opposed to the mindless regularity of popular verse? Again, the poem is not about a "measure/ resistant," it is a measure resistant. As a Klee abstract is a complete object in itself so is a Creeley poem. Reverberations occur, but in reverse of the normally understood pattern. Picture a movie of an exploding house—shown in reverse. Rather than the poem expanding out to many applications, it brings other applications into itself. The "point" of "Song" is what it is doing on the page

and what it does when it hits the ear—and mind—of the listener;
and that is presented here with precision.

II   *The Physical Object*

The pressure for precision found in Creeley's careful placement of
syllables and lines results quite understandably from a poet's in-
stinct and from a craftsman's concern for his materials; however, in
Creeley's poetry this rhythmic precision is only one part of the
larger concern with rendering the precise moment of a poem's
coming to creation. Thomas Duddy is correct when he says, in his
review of *Words*, "What Creeley is left with, and it is a unique
poetic attention, is a limitless particularity of experience in which
each moment acts out the fragmentation of time. So that the moment which the poem is *about* is indistinguishable from the moment
of the poem."[3] As we have seen in Chapter 2, Creeley attempts to
capture that moment by insisting on the sufficiency of words: they
are objects in themselves as sounds, as presences on the page, and
they need not represent some other thing. Earlier, in *Words*,
Creeley's attention focused on a similar attempt to prove the sufficiency of objects, of things. For some time he had been repeating
Williams' dictum, "No Ideas but in Things"; now he insisted,
"There is nothing/ but what thinking makes/ it less tangible," ending
that poem, "I Keep to Myself Such Measure. . .," with "I hold in
both hands such weight/ it is my only description" (52). Although
Words may be read in different ways, it can be seen in large part as
an attempt to discover and reveal the physical presence and substantiality of the object in the poem, its *dinglichtkeit*, by locating it
precisely and by scraping off abstract associations. The movement
from this concern for physical substantiality of the object in *Words*
to the physical substantiality of the word in *Pieces* then becomes
obvious and can be seen in many poems from this volume.

The link between physical object and physical language appears
overtly in the poem called "The Language." Love is by common
usage the most abstract of all words. How to make it real? How to
change "I love you," that most overused of all expressions, into
something alive? These are questions of human relationships and of
linguistics.

> Locate *I*
> *love you* some-
> where in

> teeth and
> eyes, bite
> it but
>
> take care not
> to hurt, you
> want so
>
> much so
> little. Words
> say everything,
>
> *I*
> *love you*
> again,
>
> then what
> is emptiness
> for. To
>
> fill, fill.
> I heard words
> and words full
>
> of holes
> aching. Speech
> is a mouth. (37)

As is true of Creeley's best poetry, this poem appears as simple statement but stretches out gently to touch related themes and images, creating a hovering on the page rather than a conclusion. "Speech/ is a mouth" of course emphasizes that love is made real through its presence and through its physical utterance rather than through the concept of it; actually speaking the words is a literal act and thus more real than the thought. But again (and this became even more the issue in *Pieces*) the attempt is never successful. In fact it cannot be successfully concluded because then the poem would be a static result rather than a dynamic process. The first half of the poem particularly insists on pushing and probing. Keep in mind that Creeley stops at the end of each line when reading; now notice the effect of the juncture between "bite/it," "want so/ much so/ little" before the temporary ease of "Words/ say everything" with the juncture at the normal break between subject and verb. A comparable pattern is found in the second half of the poem, beginning with "I/ love you" and ending with "Speech/ is a mouth," syntactically and thematically recalling the earlier "Words/ say everything" but intensifying that statement by switching from the abstract to the concrete. As is love, words are holes aching to be filled, a recurrent image in Creeley's poetry with its linguistic as well as its sexual associations. "The Language" then insists on the physical substantiality of literal objects (love becomes holes to be filled) and the physical substantiality of language itself (words become holes to be filled).

In poem after poem, Creeley reaches out for the substantial in the poem. In "A Place" he remembers a scene: "The wetness of that street, the light,/ the way the clouds were heavy" and then laments, "I do not feel/ what it was I was feeling." Somehow he needs to go back to that experience and not simply describe it. Finally, he must "open/ whatever door it was, find the weather/ is out there, grey, the rain then and/ now falling from the sky to the wet ground" (85). This is real, the weight of the wetness, achieved or at least approximated through a synesthetic mixture of touch, pressure, sight, and sound. In "Some Afternoon," a "world elsewhere" is rejected in favor of a world here where "the tangible faces/ smile, breaking/ into tangible pieces" (60). In a short poem, "Pieces," the pain of one person hurting another is made real by three final words, each occupying its own line: "meat/ sliced/ walking" (104). And finally, in a brief poem with the innocuous title "Hello," Creeley makes vivid the shock of human contact far beyond the average experience of that contact. The poem begins:

> With a quick
> jump he caught
> the edge of
>
> her eye and
> it tore, down,
> ripping. (40)

These and countless other examples from *Words* illustrate Creeley's reaching out for the real in the physical, a desire that he shares with many poets of this century. Creeley differs, however, in the degree of his insistence and in the frustration at what he feels is the failure of his attempt. In fact, he often uses that frustration in his poetry. His poem, "A Method," can be seen most clearly within the context of this frustration.

Patterns
of sounds, endless
discretions, whole
pauses of nouns,

clusters. This
and that, that
one, this
and that. Looking

seeing, some
thing, being
some. A piece

of cake upon,
a face, a fact, that
description like
as if then. (100)

Sound arrangements become cake on a face become fact. "A Method" suggests also the poem "For W.C.W.," which includes the lines, "There, you say, and/ there, and there,/ and *and* becomes/ just so" (27), as well as these lines from his poem "Enough": "You/ there, me/ here" (126). And even more insistently, in "The City" he says, "Again, let/ each be this or/ that, they, together," then "veg-etable,/ flower, a crazy orange/ sun, a windy/ dirt" (91). Finally, Creeley has included in *Words* several poems that baffle by their sheer minimal quality. A poem such as "The Box" seems to do nothing until it is seen as an attempt to nail the thing to the wall.

Three sides,
four
windows. Four

doors, three
hands. (116)

Out of sheer frustration, the poet seems to be pointing his finger and saying, "There, that's it. Nothing more, nothing less. Just that." A precision of focus such as that and a brazenness that can come only from frustration may have resulted in "A Piece," a poem easily ridiculed and easily misunderstood—the total poem is

> One and
> one, two
> three. (115)

—but a poem that can also be seen as the logical, perhaps inevitable extension of Creeley's doomed attempt to place the physical object on the page.

III   *The Substantial Self*

All of which leads to a corollary theme in *Words*. As Creeley attempted to substantiate physical objects, so he attempted to substantiate the self, not by looking within but by placing the self somehow outside the consciousness expressing it. In many poems in this volume Creeley refers to the self as something with a physical, independent existence, an existence just as objectively real as a tree or a house. The poet, dreamlike, is in the position of watching himself in action, as seen in these lines from "The Dream":

> In the dream
> I see
> two faces turned,
>
> one of which
> I assume mine, one
> of which I assume. (53)

The experience described in this poem and others is quite common. We have all at one time or another, waking or dreaming, seen ourselves as though we were an outsider or observer; however, within the thesis being developed in this chapter, the recording of this phenomenon by Creeley can be seen as another extension of his doomed attempt to fix the physical object (in this case the self) on the page. If a tree or a house has a physical presence that can be at least in part captured, why not the self? And how else to do it than to capture a moment in time—a concern that became much more prominent in *Pieces*. The poem "The Measure" begins with a realization of the self's predicament in time:

> I cannot
> move backward
> or forward.
> I am caught
>
> in time
> as measure. (45)

While in "Walking":

> In my head I am
> walking but I am not
> in my head (36).

In still other poems the split between the consciousness producing the poem and the self is made even more overt, as in an early
part of the poem "A Sight":

> *He/I*
> were walking. Then
> the place *is/was*
> not ever enough. (101)

or even more strikingly in the outwardly autobiographical poem,
"I," which begins with the title and continues "is the grandson of
Thomas L. Creeley," thereby making of the first person pronoun a
third person noun as though "I" were the name of Thomas L.
Creeley's grandson. This device produces a curiously disjointed impression of the self, especially since he keeps the first person posses-
sive elsewhere in the poem.

> I, is late

> But I saw a picture of him once, T.L.
> in a chair in Belmont, or it was his invalid
> and patient wife they told me sat there, he
> was standing, long and steady faced,
> a burden to him she was, and the son. The
> other child had died
> They waited, so my father
> who also died when I is four gave all
> to something like
> the word "adjoined," "extended"
> so I feels

> I sees the time as long and wavering
> grass in all about the lot in all that
> cemetery again the old man owned a part of
> so they couldn't dig him up. (33–34)

In this poem the third person "I" creates a greater sense of objectivity, a viewing the thing out there, separate, hence in a better position to be analyzed. In another poem, however, the "I" is split into an outside-inside relationship, creating complex connections between the two "I's" and thus allowing Creeley to say something with greater precision than if he had stayed with the single "I." The poem titled "The Pattern," begins:

> As soon as
> I speak, I
> speaks. It
>
> wants to
> be free but
> impassive lies
>
> in the direction
> of its
> words. (49)

Creeley here separates the self into the man ("I speak") and the poet ("I speaks"), allowing the man to comment on the poet as a third person object ("It/ wants to/ be free"). He is obviously describing the role of the poet, which is as a third party agent to the creative process. The poem arrives through its own insistence upon the poet who "lies [in two senses of the word] in the direction/ of its/ words." This passive function is presented dramatically by splitting the poet's self in two and having one observe the other.

IV   *Love and Loneliness*

And finally, to feelings, or more specifically love, a major subject of the poems in *Words*, as in all of Creeley's writing. How to make a vague, elusive emotion precise and tangible? In "The Language" the words "I love you" became real, but what about the feelings behind those words? Here we come back again to rhythmic precision. In a poem titled "Song," Creeley asks a difficult question with an even more difficult answer, an answer—or at least its difficulty—suggested by the *way* the question is asked.

What do you
want, love. To be
loved. What,

what wanted,
love, (79)

Once more the heavy end stops provide the crucial play between
normal syntax and the poet's insistent voice. The simple desire to be
loved is impossible to know until the feeling becomes not abstract
words but "a simple/ recognition," and, finally, the feeling and recognition are stripped bare becoming "two things,/ one and one."
Hesitant insistence also marks a poem called "Going," which begins, "There is nothing/ to turn from,/ or to, no/ way other/ than
forward." The line breaks correspond to syntactical junctures except, crucially, between "no" and "way" (a break between stanzas
also occurs here), the result being a phrase broken in two and
hanging suspended for the moment. The poem ends with a similar
pattern, but softer this time as a degree of reconciliation is achieved:
"Let me/ leave here a/ mark, a/ way through/ her mind" (90). These
soft hesitancies are used most effectively in a poem Creeley wrote to
his wife, Bobbie, which demonstrates how subtly he modulates his
voice through rhythmic precision.

What can occur
invests the weather, also
but the trees, again,
are in bloom.

The day will not
be less than that. I
am writing to you,
wishing to be rid of

these confusions. You
have so largely
let me continue, not
as indulgence but

then to say I
have said, and will,
anything is so
hard, at this moment.

> In my mind, as
> ever, you occur. Your
> face is such
> delight, I can
>
> see the lines there
> as the finest
> mark of ourselves.
> Your skin at moments
>
> is translucent. I
> want to make love
> to you, now. The world
> is the trees, you,
>
> I cannot change it,
> the weather
> occurs, the mind
> is not its only witness. (97–98)

Briefly, this poem speaks of loneliness and of love overcoming that loneliness. The woman becomes real "in my mind" as the trees bloom, as "the weather/ occurs." But the poem is much more than this. Somehow Creeley manages to capture that precise configuration of reaching out, touching and not touching—physical separation diminished by love but not completely destroyed by it. Both love and loneliness remain, and in precise ratio to each other, a ratio achieved by mixing easy syntax with occasional slightly less normal line breaks. The first five lines, for instance, follow normal syntactical grouping. Line six, however, ends with the first word of a new sentence, "I" sitting there alone, a pause, and then the release into the next line. Stanza four comments on the difficulty of the moment's loneliness in awkward rhythms and slightly disjointed syntax, followed by the simple statement of the next stanza, the image returning "In my mind, as/ ever."

V   *The Critical Reception*

This is the artist's complete control over his material, consciously and instinctively. In fact, such poetry approaches at least what Creeley apparently intended in this volume, to make the *way* of the poem and not the matter the point to be demonstrated. In 1960 Creeley had written, "I mean then *words*—as opposed to content. I care what the poem says, only as a poem—I am no longer interested in the exterior attitude to which the poem may well point, as signpost. . . ."[4] A simple concept certainly, a concept obviously used by painters such as the abstract expressionists (Franz Kline had said, "Painting is paint," and Creeley approved), by contemporary minimal sculptors, and by composers, in fact almost always by composers; but a concept causing much controversy in Creeley criticism. Many of the reservations in the reviews of *Words* might be traced to a misunderstanding of this concept. John Thompson, for instance, writing in the *New York Review of Books*, refers to these poems as abstract and general, appealing to "soft, naive, dreamy readers";[5] while Ronald Hayman, reviewing the English publication of *Poems 1950–1965*, which contained the first two-thirds of *Words*, called these poems insubstantial and mannered.[6] At least two reviewers left no mistake about their dislike for *Words*. Peter Davison, writing in the *Atlantic Monthly*, said:

His earlier poems, though limited in range, displayed subtlety of sound and intricacy of feeling. In *Words* his range has narrowed to the vanishing point, and his energy has subsided almost into catatonia. These poems are so exiguous, so limited in emotion, language, and movement as to be hardly perceptible. . . . Creeley's new work announces the victory of the inarticulate. A battle against glibness has been won, but at a terrible price: almost all the organs of language have been removed. These poems vary neither in tone, in form, in imagery, nor in intention. . . . Creeley's poetry has reached a dead end of self-limitation. . . ."[7]

And John Perreault in the *New York Times Book Review* lamented the direction of Creeley's verse:

In what appears to be his search for greater purity, clarity and efficiency of language, he has almost completely eliminated the freshness of viewpoint that occasionally enlivened his earlier efforts. The same subjects remain: personalized versions of love, pain, sex and death, but whittled down to "breath units" of often breathless banality. Sometimes, it must be admitted, the thinness of vision and the absence of imagination is effectively disguised by what can only be described as esthetic control. . . .[8]

Most reviewers, however, saw what Creeley was attempting to do, even if they did not always approve of the attempt. Louis Simpson said in *Harper's Magazine* that in *Words* "everything is style; there is no subject but the poem talking to itself. Such visible objects as were present in his early poems are missing here. These are syllables, breathing pauses, whispers."[9] True, but one senses here a note of regret. No regret is suggested, however, in reviews such as G. S. Fraser's brief, complimentary note in *Partisan Review*,[10] or in Donald Junkins' review in which he called *Words* "an extraordinarily fine book," observing that "the setting is . . . the mind itself, and the poems are conceptual, nonimagistic, anti-romantic."[11] And still other reviews both praised the book and noted Creeley's accomplishment. Thomas A. Duddy observed that "Creeley's poems act out the hesitancy of their own coming to be and serve as reminders of the silence they are situated in."[12] This view of a Creeley poem as process in action, or energy construct as Olson said, is echoed in one other highly favorable review in *Poetry*, always receptive to Creeley. Frederic Will sees *Words* as a group of poems hovering on the point of just having been made: "They all both are, and are about, the surprise, quality, and finality of coming into being, of occupying the unique point at which the poem has just arrested itself," concluding that this volume "marks a new moment in twentieth century American poetry."[13]

High praise, but even more important, valid observation of the poems in *Words*. Creeley has moved to a greater precision of rhythm than in his earlier poems and has exhibited a greater faith in the *way* of the poem to prove its effect. Matter is still here but is pared more to the minimal, anticipating the poems of *Pieces* and beyond. Creeley himself saw where he had been and where he was going in 1965: "Still, it was never what they [poems] said *about* things that interested me. I wanted a poem itself to exist and that could never be possible as long as some subject significantly elsewhere was involved. There had to be an independence derived from the very fact that words are things too."[14] Words as things became a major theme in Creeley's later poems; here those words are used to attempt the impossible: to fix the object, the self, even love, wriggling to the page.

CHAPTER 4

For Love

IN *Pieces* Creeley arrived at his goal, or at least as close to it as is linguistically possible: The word became a physical object in a frozen moment of time. The razor edge upon which many of these poems rest is seen too in *Words*, where one of Creeley's main preoccupations is with the physical substantiality of the object, its "thingness." In both volumes, precision is the key factor, precision of diction, precision of rhythms, precision of images. So too in *For Love, Poems 1950–1960*, but in still another sense, for this volume, Creeley's first collection, impresses one less with the minimal technique of his later poetry, although the origins are here, than with his thematic concern for the relationships between people. Creeley was first known as a poet of love—and hate—as a poet of the fragile point of contact between people; and he expressed these feelings with disarming understatement and precise perception. Most critics and reviewers of *For Love* saw instantly the constant examination of this precarious edge of human relationships. Peter Davison in *Atlantic,* despite certain reservations about "incorrect" grammar and punctuation, commented:

Creeley has a subtle, almost feminine sensibility, and the best of his poems are those dealing with the intricacies that exist between men and women. The poems move back and forth between the mood of loneliness on the one hand and on the other the repeated exhortation, "Be natural." The poems fulfill this plea in their plaintiveness, their refusal to oversimplify, in their aloneness, even in their mannerisms. They evade the bold statement, luxuriate in the inconclusive, and often strike perfectly the note of the dying fall.[1]

Paul Carroll in *Nation* was even more explicit: "Creeley is, above all, a poet of immediate, concrete, personal relationships—between lovers, friends, a man with himself. Landscape, weather, architec-

ture, human appearances have no place in his work except as
backdrop—and then only rarely—for the particular relationship
being embodied in the poem."[2] This too is what young readers
responded to in Creeley's poetry. Love was treated openly, honestly, unashamedly, and without the idyllic overlay provided by the
mass media and popular culture. When one commits oneself to
another, he guarantees himself a degree of happiness, but he also
guarantees himself a degree of pain. Creeley accepted and revealed
both in intensely personal poems.

What most reviewers did not see in *For Love*, however, was *how*
these poems work; they saw what these poems were saying, but not
the "way" they spoke. And it is precisely this way, this precision of
technique, that Creeley was to carry along and refine in the subsequent volumes of *Words* and *Pieces*. Certain reviewers, surpris-
ingly, saw no precision at all. D. J. Hughes said in the *Massachusetts Review* that the first two sections especially "consist of
botched fragments, brief pantings which would be poetically necessary if they could,"[3] echoing the sentiments of Ralph J. Mills, reviewing *A Form of Women* (1959), one of the small volumes collected in *For Love*. Creeley's poems, he said, were characterized by
"flippancy and carelessness of composition, the unsupported vagueness of poetic events that are wanting in materials and technique."[4]
Creeley's later poetry was to reveal the inaccuracy of these observations; however, to many readers of Creeley's early verse, his poems
could easily be seen as intentionally confusing: ellipses and disjointed syntax could be seen as carelessness; tautness could be seen
as shallowness; and the short, breathless lines could be seen, in the
words of one British reviewer, as "thin monologues [straggling]
down the page, pointlessly chopped into 3- or 4-line stanzas . . . ."[5]

But poets, especially, saw what Creeley was doing technically,
perhaps because they were already familiar with his poetry and with
him. Paul Carroll's observations have already been mentioned.
Robert Duncan simply assumed Creeley's importance and placed
these poems in a long tradition of love poetry.[6] Stanley Kunitz
called Creeley the best of a school of "Actualists"—poets who are
determined to record the fact strictly and sparely.[7] But the most
remarkable and, in light of Creeley's later poetry, the most perceptive, article was published in *Poetry*—consistently Creeley's most
important supporter—written by Frederick Eckman as a review of
the short 1956 volume, *All That Is Lovely in Men*. Stating flatly that

"Creeley is, in my opinion, the best poet under forty now writing," Eckman went on to describe those qualities in Creeley's poetry that later readers would learn to know and to understand.

> With Robert Creeley the fragments and lacunae are always intentional, part of a deliberate strategy. . . . He is . . . the most *conserving* poet I know; he wastes nothing—in fact, at times, rather too little. Creeley's poems are characterized by constriction, the partially revealed vision, economy of utterance—to a degree that would be very nearly a fault, were it not for his exquisite sense of the collapsed rhythm, the precisely right degree of flatness, the stabbing flicker of wit: almost a negation of poetry in the act of poetry. Creeley is a desperate man, artistically speaking, a purist's purist who utters not one grunt more than he actually knows, releases no sound that his voice has not tasted.[8]

Eckman's contention that Creeley's "collapsed rhythm" and "flatness" are intentional and precariously right for his poetry returns us to the occasion of many early Creeley poems, that love-hate relationship, with its accompanying happiness-pain, and to Creeley's ability to examine those relationships with deft precision of word and emotion.

Again, in *Pieces* the word became flesh; in *Words* the object became real ("No Ideas but in Things"); and before that, in *For Love*, emotions were examined so closely and with such vulnerable honesty that they too for many readers became real. The emotion examined most often is love—and its other side, loneliness—which gives both theme and structure to the book. *For Love*, as the subtitle indicates, includes poems written over a ten year span during which several experiences caused Creeley's attitude toward love to change or perhaps to evolve, an evolution reflected in the content and to some extent the form of the poems. By the middle of the 1950s, Creeley's first marriage had ended after several years of considerable friction. During the last years of this marriage and for a time thereafter, Creeley's poems presented a satiric, even sarcastic, and certainly guarded view of love and marriage, and a skepticism of human relationships generally. Early in 1957, Creeley met and married Bobbie Hall, events that changed his life and, gradually, his poetry, because from that point to the end of *For Love*, the poems become much more sympathetic to the viability of love, and even marriage, and much more relaxed in themselves. The movement, however, is complicated further by one other fact of Creeley's life.

His unsuccessful marriage had demonstrated to him not only the bankruptcy of genuine emotion but also what seemed to be an irreconcilable conflict between the vocation of the artist and the ordinary demands of marriage and family, a realization further strengthened by his reading of *The White Goddess* by Robert Graves, who was residing on Mallorca when Creeley was there. According to Graves the muse demands all; domesticity is its arch enemy. In these curious, transitional poems between the failure of love and its success in Bobbie, Creeley appears to be working out his version of Grave's dilemma.

I   *The Unsure Egoist*

But first, the poems by which Creeley was first known and that continue to be associated with his name—the cynical, at times humorous, at times bitter "love-hate" poetry of the first half of *For Love*, and the values that such poetry postulates. In his earliest published poems, collected in *For Love*, Creeley explicitly describes the world as he sees it—a world without substance and without meaning, a world devoid of all except—and this "except" is vital because his poetry can be seen primarily as an amplification of this "except"—human relationships. Creeley examines the double nature of human relationships: on one hand this is all the individual has to protect him against the void, while on the other hand commitment to such relationships necessarily involves pain and suffering. The title poem of an earlier volume, "The Immoral Proposition," put this bluntly and then pursued the implications with finer distinctions.

> If you never do anything for anyone else
> you are spared the tragedy of human relation-
>
> ships. If quietly and like another time
> there is the passage of an unexpected thing:
>
> to look at it is more
> than it was. God knows
>
> nothing is competent nothing is
> all there is. The unsure
>
> egoist is not
> good for himself.[9]

The first two lines plus one syllable (which breaks "relationship" in two as later "unsure egoist" is broken in two) summarizes Camus or Sartre neatly, simplistically, and prosaically. Certainly here the diction is flat and the rhythms those of a textbook. The second section, however, begins to slide in tone toward an assertion less definite, less confident, and yet consistent with the first assertion. Sections three and four appear to contradict each other, heightening the impression of lack of confidence; however, they do not literally contradict each other, since to remember something that happened unexpectedly is to remember both more and less than actually happened. The "unsure/egoist" then assumes an interesting and entirely appropriate ambiguity, since he (the poet as well as the man) sees the world only in terms of his relationship to members of that world—and yet he must hesitate, waver, because those relationships can be painful. Creeley thus takes a flat, platitudinous assertion to its unique (it can only be that for the egoist) conclusion, the movement being from sureness to unsureness, with the tone of the poem shifting accordingly.

The unsure egoist is man trying to come to terms with his world, but he is also the poet trying to come to terms with his function within that world. In another poem, "The Dishonest Mailmen," written slightly earlier, Creeley uses tone to save his statement, and in the process comments on the poet and the world he inhabits.

> They are taking all my letters, and they
> put them into a fire.
>
> >I see the flames, etc.
> But do not care, etc.
>
> They burn everything I have, or what little
> I have. I don't care, etc.
>
> The poem supreme, addressed to
> emptiness—this is the courage
>
> necessary. This is something
> quite different. (29)

Creeley combines a casual diction, highlighted by the "etc.'s," with a pompous statement, "The poem supreme, addressed to/ emptiness—this is the courage/ necessary," and concludes with a return to the casual. "This is something" appears to continue the affected heroism of the "poem supreme," but instead the line drops down to a disarming "quite different." The pretense ends, the mailmen really do care what happens to their letters but are unsure enough of themselves not to admit it.

Creeley's love poems, then, or more properly his relationship poems (a terrible, immemorable phrase) consist at this stage of desperate, halting attempts at human contact with an instinctive awareness that one has to protect himself against being hurt in the process. All he has between himself and nothingness is this fragile link with others. And this is precisely how Creeley has seen the function of his poetry, from then until now—a fragile link with others. Little wonder that his poems reveal a halting precision and a belief in the value of the attempt, the achievement being beyond the possible.

The poems of the first section of *For Love*, written between 1950 and 1955, reflect, especially those during 1953 and 1954, a disillusionment with love and marriage that is almost total, a result in part at least of his own deteriorating marriage.[10] These poems refer constantly to the bankruptcy of marriage with a devastating rancor, bitterness, and directness. "The Crisis" written early in 1952, begins: "Let me say (in anger) that since the day we were married/ we have never had a towel/ where anyone could find it,/ the fact" (19). In two poems written in 1953, Creeley defines first the emptiness of his marriage: "My involvement is just an old/ habitual relationship./ cruel, cruel to describe/ what there is no reason to describe" (34), and then the effect on himself: "When I know what people think of me/ I am plunged into my loneliness" (39). By spring of 1954 Creeley wrote a "Song" fantasizing divorce, desiring out. Were he "more blithe," he says, he "would tear up all the checks/ made out to me,/ not giving a good goddamn/ what the hell happened" (48). Even in these few lines one can see that Creeley is playing the romantic idylic conventions of the song against the flat, prosaic rhythms and diction of angry speech. The disdain produced by mockery of a convention is transferred to mockery of what that convention represents: the supreme value of romantic love. And this contempt continued through the poems of 1955, as in "Naughty Boy," a poem that shows the wife totally misunderstanding the husband. The poem begins, "When he brings home a whale,/ she laughs and says, that's not for real./ And if he won the Irish sweepstakes,/ she would say, where were you last night?" (49). Contempt appears in "The Business" also, but with a slight modification. Love can occur, although the risk of being hurt is high, becoming finally "a remote chance/ on which you stake/ yourself" (44).

The poems of the first half of Section Two (1956–1958) continue this skepticism of love and attack on marriage. Some, as "A Marriage," describe matter of factly Creeley's own marriage.

> The first retainer
> he gave to her
> was a golden
> wedding ring.
>
> The second—late at night
> he woke up,
> leaned over on an elbow,
> and kissed her.
>
> The third and the last—
> he died with
> and gave up loving
> and lived with her. (74)

Others, however, mocked literary conventions, following the line of "Song," discussed above. In a long and well-known poem, "Ballad of the Despairing Husband," Creeley reverses the tradition of courtly love, in the process all but destroying the lady to whom the poem is directed. His wife has left him, ending a marriage ambiguous at best ("I fought with her, she fought with me"), but nevertheless good as seen through the eyes of the supposedly naive narrator ("And things went on right merrily"). Throughout the poem Creeley juxtaposes the narrator's simple love and the wife's coarse response. Stanza three is typical:

> Oh come home soon, I write to her.
> Go screw yourself, is her answer.
> Now what is that, for Christian word?
> I hope she feeds on dried goose turd. (76)

Ladies in ballads simply do not speak like that (and simple-minded narrators do not rhyme "Christian word" with "dried goose turd"). The result is humorous, but more than that it is bitter mockery. The long conclusion to the poem, an apparently endless and absurd invocation to the lady, combines naiveté and mocking tones with the equally contrasting tribute to the lady and the conscious ineptitude of the poet as the lines flatten themselves into aimlessly meandering banalities.

Oh lovely lady, morning or evening or afternoon.
Oh lovely lady, eating with or without a spoon.
Oh most lovely lady, whether dressed or undressed or partly.
Oh most lovely lady, getting up or going to bed or sitting only.

Oh loveliest of ladies, than whom none is more fair, more
          gracious, more beautiful
Oh loveliest of ladies, whether you are just or unjust,
          merciful, indifferent, or cruel.
Oh most loveliest of ladies, doing whatever, seeing whatever,
          being whatever.
Oh most loveliest of ladies, in rain, in shine, in any weather.

Oh lady, grant me time,
please, to finish my rhyme. (77)

The result is devastating, because while the assumed but unspoken truth of courtly poetry is that the lady is there so that the poet has an occasion for his poetry, in this poem that assumption becomes the literal truth: he never did take the lady seriously. This is the final humiliation, and behind the humor of the poem lies a sensibility totally suspicious of permanent relationships.

Although none of the other poems of *For Love* approach "Ballad of the Despairing Husband" as mockery, several consciously parody earlier poems. "The Bed," for instance, takes off on Byron, beginning: "She walks in beauty like a lake/ and eats her steak/ with fork and knife/ and proves a proper wife" (66); and "Just Friends" parodies Whitman's poem with its opening lines: "Out of the table endlessly rocking,/ sea-shells, and firm,/ I saw a face appear/ which called me dear" (67). The effect of these parodies, as of "Ballad," is to ridicule and hence make useless the values held by the originals. Here and elsewhere in these early poems, the message is clear: Marriage offers little hope against the void. In fact, there seems little hope at all, except perhaps in the painful probing of poetry itself. Creeley had said during these years, "You send me your poems,/ I'll send you mine./ Things tend to awaken/ even through random communication" (37); but this voice is not heard often through the first half of *For Love*.

II *The Lady*

Then during the later years of the decade, Creeley's poetry began to change, a change that Creeley himself had recognized in an interview with David Ossman in May 1961. "Now the truncated line, or the short, seemingly broken line I was using in my first poems, comes from the somewhat broken emotions that were involved in them. Now, as I begin to relax, as I not so much grow older, but more settled, more at ease in my world, the line can not so much grow softer, but can become, as you say, more lyrical, less afraid of concluding."[11] He began to be more relaxed, more at ease in his world, his emotions less broken. And this ease is reflected in his line and in his changing attitudes toward permanent relationships, a change directly attributable to his marriage early in 1957 to his second wife, Bobbie. Allen B. Cameron saw this change when writing of *For Love* in 1967; Creeley is moving "in this last section . . . from hopefulness and evasion to certainty and lasting possession of the past."[12] Creeley's friend Robert Duncan wrote even more revealingly of this transition. Duncan said first that Creeley's poems are clearly within the tradition of courtly love, suggesting that *For Love* continues a line from Dante through Cavalcant's "Donna Mi Prega," Provençal love poetry, Rosetti in the last century, and portions of Pound's *Cantos* in this century. The list is suggestive rather than definitive; the point, however, is clear and accurate. Creeley is distinguishing in these poems, as does the convention of courtly love, between the woman to whom he is married and the woman to whom he owes his ultimate allegiance and to whom he dedicates his endeavors. Duncan supports his contention by pointing out that Creeley paraphrases Dante's reference to Beatrice ("La gloriosa donna della mia mente"—"the glorious lady of my mind"—in *La Vita Nuova*) in his reference to the other woman of "The Whip" ("the other in my mind/ occurs").[13]

But Duncan goes on to suggest that Creeley is relying on another tradition in these poems, a tradition involving myth, in which the woman becomes more completely the muse who provides both pleasure and pain to her devotee, who permits him to reach the highest peaks of existence but who also can and probably will destroy him. Although Duncan does not pursue this idea in Creeley's poems as far as he might, he does drop one more hint: a useful relationship might be seen between Creeley's poems involving "the women who are power" (Duncan's phrase) and Robert Graves' *The White God-*

dess.[14] Creeley knew Graves slightly when both were living in
Mallorca during the early 1950s and knew the book; in fact, he
began a review of several new editions of Swinburne's poems by
quoting Graves' description of the goddess, a description he himself
had used in earlier poems: "The Goddess is a lovely, slender woman
with a hooked nose, deathly pale face, lips as red as rowan-berries,
startlingly blue eyes and long fair hair; she will suddenly transform
herself into sow, mare, bitch, vixen, she-ass, weasel, serpent, owl,
she-wolf, tigress, mermaid or loathsome hag. . . ."[15] The White
Goddess, according to Graves' brilliant and controversial account, is
the source of creation, the Earth-Mother, in any of her mythical and
physical manifestations. All men owe her allegiance, but the poet
has a special duty because she is his muse. Toward the end of *The
White Goddess*, Graves makes clear his reasons for the failure of
most modern poetry.

But perhaps also he has lost his sense of the White Goddess [synonymous
with Truth]: the woman he took to be a Muse, or who was a Muse, turns
into a domestic woman and would have him turn similarly into a domesticated man. Loyalty prevents him from parting company with her, especially
if she is the mother of his children and is proud to be reckoned a good
housewife; and as the Muse fades out, so does the poet. . . . The White
Goddess is anti-domestic; she is the perpetual "other woman," and her part
is difficult indeed for a woman of sensibility to play for more than a few
years. . . .[16]

Even as early as 1954, Creeley appears to be wrestling with the
art-domesticity dilemma in terms of two women, each with separate
demands on him. "The Whip" begins:

> I spent a night turning in bed,
> my love was a feather, a flat
>
> sleeping thing. She was
> very white
>
> and quiet, and above us on
> the roof, there was another woman I
>
> also loved, had
> addressed myself to in
>
> a fit she
> returned. (51)

Compare these lines with the clearer, more definite statement of "The Wife," written five years later, after his marriage to Bobbie and after he had satisfactorily answered the question posed in the poem.

> I know two women
>   and the one
> is tangible substance,
>   flesh and bone.
>
> The other in my mind
>   occurs.
> She keeps her strict
>   proportion there.
>
> But how should I
>   propose to live
> with two such creatures
>   in my bed—
>
> or how shall he
>   who has a wife
> yield two to one
>   and watch the other die. (154)

The answer Creeley finally arrived at was that he could have both the muse and the domestic woman. Bobbie demonstrated that one woman could serve both functions, but that realization and that acceptance did not come easily to Creeley. The two years following his marriage show Creeley hesitantly beginning to accept love once more as, in his poem "The Song," when he says "It still makes sense/ to know the song after all" (117), although he still had fears:

> No woman ever was,
> was wiser
> than you. None is
> more true.
>
> But fate, love, fate
> scares me. (128)

The movement is clear; with all his doubts and scars, Creeley is moving from cynicism to acceptance, helped along at least in part by dividing woman into muse and wife before reuniting them in Bobbie. A key poem in this transition—and one that can be understood

clearly only within this context—is "The Door," written early in
1959 and, significantly, dedicated to Robert Duncan, but placed
near the end of the second section, the poems of 1956–1958.

It is hard going to the door
cut so small in the wall where
the vision which echoes loneliness
brings a scent of wild flowers in a wood.

What I understood, I understand.
My mind is sometime torment,
sometimes good and filled with livelihood,
and feels the ground.

But I see the door,
and knew the wall, and wanted the wood,
and would get there if I could
with my feet and hands and mind.

Lady, do not banish me
for digressions. My nature
is a quagmire of unresolved
confessions. Lady, I follow.

I walked away from myself,
I left the room, I found the garden,
I knew the woman
in it, together we lay down.

Dead night remembers. In December
we change, not multiplied but dispersed,
sneaked out of childhood,
the ritual of dismemberment.

Mighty magic is a mother,
in her there is another issue
of fixture, repeated form, the race renewal,
the change of the command.

The garden echoes across the room.
It is fixed in the wall like a mirror
that faces a window behind you
and reflects the shadows.

May I go now?
Am I allowed to bow myself down
in the ridiculous posture of renewal,
of the insistence of which I am the virtue?

Nothing for You is untoward.
Inside You would also be tall,
more tall, more beautiful.
Come toward me from the wall, I want to be with You.

So I screamed to You,
who hears as the wind, and changes
multiply, invariably,
changes in the mind.

Running to the door, I ran down
as a clock runs down. Walked backwards,
stumbled, sat down
hard on the floor near the wall.

Where were You.
How absurd, how vicious.
There is nothing to do but get up.
My knees were iron, I rusted in worship, of You.

For that one sings, one
writes the spring poem, one goes on walking.
The Lady has always moved to the next town
and you stumble on after Her.

The door in the wall leads to the garden
where in the sunlight sit
the Graces in long Victorian dresses,
of which my grandmother had spoken.

History sings in their faces.
They are young, they are obtainable,
and you follow after them also
in the service of God and Truth.

But the Lady is indefinable,
she will be the door in the wall
to the garden in sunlight.
I will go on talking forever.

I will never get there.
Oh Lady, remember me
who in Your service grows older
not wiser, no more than before.

How can I die alone.
Where will I be then who am now alone,
what groans so pathetically
in this room where I am alone?

> I will go to the garden.
> I will be a romantic. I will sell
> myself in hell,
> in heaven also I will be.
>
> In my mind I see the door,
> I see the sunlight before me across the floor
> beckon to me, as the Lady's skirt
> moves small beyond it. (101–103)

Upon a first reading of the poem, the tendency is to see the Lady as a woman, the object of a traditional love poem. The poet is flattering her, telling her how much he needs her, asking for her favors; but almost immediately one senses a difference here. The Lady is capitalized (even the pronoun referring to her is capitalized, suggesting a deification), the diction is relatively elevated, and much of the poem remains a mystery. Why the persistence of the garden through the door? Why the wavering on the part of the speaker? Why the seasonal reference? Each question, and many more, might be answered simply by saying he wants to convince the woman of his love, but all together they suggest more than that. Think of the Lady in Graves' sense as the muse who demands total homage, and think of other manifestations of the goddess, particularly as used by the ancient Greeks. Such a view of "The Door" is strengthened further by the poem, "Kore," also written in 1959, in which Creeley used the myth of Kore/ Persephone, daughter of Demeter, the goddess of agriculture and a version of the White Goddess. Persephone was stolen by Hades, king of the underworld, and returned to a mourning Demeter only after Demeter's grief caused her to neglect the fields and produce the consequent famine. Persephone could return, but with one condition. While with Hades, she ate one pomegranate seed; thus she must spend one third of the year in the underworld. The myth accounts for the barren Greek fields between the harvest in early summer and the rains and planting of autumn, but on a deeper level, it reflects the turning of the seasons with the accompanying birth, death, and rebirth cycle. The return of Persephone from the underworld (the grain was literally stored underground during the hot, barren summer months) is the return of life, and as the goddess-muse, it is the return of the poet's true vocation.

The Lady of "The Door" is then the goddess-muse whose garden-woods contain both the smell of wild flowers and loneliness and whose worshipper is the poet. Total commitment to the muse is difficult but necessary, and the poet continually wavers between accepting his role and acknowledging the impossibility of his effort. Near the end of the poem he says, "I will never get there," and two stanzas later he says with equal resolve, "I will go to the garden." He is unsure, lacking confidence in the presence of the Lady whose garden is both accessible and inaccessible. Early in the poem he says, "Lady, I follow," ending the poem with the image of following the Lady across the room, through the door, and into the sunlight. Furthermore, Creeley ties in the muse as the source of true artistic fecundity with the goddess as the source of all life, represented by the turning of the seasons. In stanza five the speaker tells of how he left the room to lie with the woman and then undergoes the ritual of dismemberment in the "dead night" of December in stanza six, followed by the "race renewal" of stanza seven, clearly a reference to new life ("repeated forms"). These stanzas parallel the story of the goddess, who chooses a compatriot to lie with her in June, and then in December he is sacrificed, dismembered, and even eaten to insure the fertility of the soil and the constant renewal of the race. Creeley combines worship of the muse with the concept of regeneration, both literally and through art, and feeling some embarrassment at his own pretentiousness. All of this combines in the lines of stanza nine, "Am I allowed to bow myself down/ in the ridiculous posture of renewal," an image of worship and of intercourse.

The poem reverberates endlessly, but the point is clear: The poet will be a romantic, remembering that the term itself is for Graves synonymous with the true muse-poet.

III   *Be Natural*

This resolution is only temporary, however, because soon or even simultaneously Creeley worked out what for Graves remained the irreconcilable conflict between art and domesticity, because Creeley realized that in Bobbie art and domesticity could cohabit. The poems of part three of *For Love,* especially those toward the end, relax into themselves. Even those poems not involving Bobbie directly suggest an ease, represented in the phrase used several times by Creeley, "Be natural." In a poem called, as so many of Creeley's poems are, "Song," the new start is clear in the opening stanza:

> Those rivers run from that land
> to sea. The wind
> finds trees to move,
> then goes again. (132)

His advice here is to himself:

> Be natural, while alive.
> Dead, we die to that
> also, and go another
> course, I hope. (132)

Natural as the wind is to the trees or to water, and this is the advice
he gives to his daughter in "The Name," a poem discussed in Chapter 6: "Be natural,/ wise/ as you can be,/ my daughter" (144). Natural
in the sense that the parts fit and that the forms are completed, the
impulse followed. Natural, too, in the sense that art is produced by
its own insistence, as in "The House":

> Mud put
> upon mud,
> lifted
> to make room,
>
> house
> a cave,
> and
> colder night.
>
> To sleep
> in, live in,
> to come in
> from heat,
>
> all form derived
> from kind,
> built
> with that in mind. (139)

"All form derived/ from kind" directly states the organic concept of
art ("form is never more than an extension of . content" and "form is
what happens") and, incidentally, the organic concept of life.
Creeley had managed toward the end of the 1950s to combine his

poetry and his personal life successfully and easily and, largely
through the presence of Bobbie, to reconcile these two impulses.

The resolution appears gently, surely, in the first stanza of "Love
Comes Quietly."

> Love comes quietly,
> finally, drops
> about me, on me,
> in the old ways. (151)

The form of this stanza captures perfectly the relaxed completedness
of love come once more. Lines one and four state the theme directly
in balanced, complete phrases. Line two juxtaposes "finally" and
"drops" with "about me" dropping to the next line, which itself
catches and balances the parallel phrases "about me" and "on me."
The lines are easily and confidently precise. But it is in the two
longer poems dedicated to Bobbie, "The Rose" and "For Love,"
that the full complexity of this resolution can be seen. Each moves
through doubt and suspicion to final, effortless acceptance of love as
an answer to the void, mirroring the movement of the volume itself.

Throughout the first two-thirds of "The Rose," the tone is uncer-
tain: "Did you want/ to go, then why/ don't you" contains a sharp
edge; a certain place has "grown monstrous"; even "her nature/ [is]
to him, vague and unsure" (148). But then the transformation occurs, recorded in the last three stanzas of the poem.

> And as if,
> as if a cloud had
> broken at last
> open
>
> and all the rain
> from that,
> from that had fallen
> on them,
>
> on them there is a mark
> of her nature, her flowers,
> and his room, his nature,
> to come home to. (149)

The vague, unsure nature of the woman and the rose become substantial, easily, through the purifying rainfall, and the poet returns to himself. Undoubtedly, Creeley has in mind here an association between Dante's Beatrice and Bobbie, since the rose is Dante's symbol for Beatrice in the *Paradiso*. As Beatrice served to guide Dante on the last part of his journey, so the rose becomes the firm substance on which the poet can rely.

Finally, the poem that provides the title *For Love* and that concludes the volume is also the poem that most clearly outlines the poet's movement toward a reconciliation of the muse-domesticity dilemma in Bobbie.

> Yesterday I wanted to
> speak of it, that sense above
> the others to me
> important because all
>
> that I know derives
> from what it teaches me.
> Today, what is it that
> is finally, so helpless,
>
> different, despairs of its own
> statement, wants to
> turn away, endlessly
> to turn away.
>
> If the moon did not . . .
> no, if you did not
> I wouldn't either, but
> what would I not
>
> do, what prevention, what
> thing so quickly stopped.
> That is love yesterday
> or tomorrow, not
>
> now. Can I eat
> what you give me. I
> have not earned it. Must
> I think of everything

as earned. Now love also
becomes a reward so
remote from me I have
only made it with my mind.

Here is tedium,
despair, a painful
sense of isolation and
whimsical if pompous

self-regard. But that image
is only of the mind's
vague structure, vague to me
because it is my own.

Love, what do I think
to say. I cannot say it.
What have you become to ask,
what have I made you into,

companion, good company,
crossed legs with skirt, or
soft body under
the bones of the bed.

Nothing says anything
but that which it wishes
would come true, fears
what else might happen in

some other place, some
other time not this one.
A voice in my place, an
echo of that only in yours.

Let me stumble into
not the confession but
the obsession I begin with
now. For you

also (also)
some time beyond place, or
place beyond time, no
mind left to

> say anything at all,
> that face gone, now.
> Into the company of love
> it all returns. (159–60)

Even here in the company of love, doubts linger and will continue to linger. Nothing is certain for tomorrow, yesterday is gone, only the present moment is real; and, perhaps, just perhaps, that is enough. Almost as though he were consciously rejecting the goddess herself, he corrects his statement, "If the moon did not . . ./ no, if you did not," the moon being another form of the goddess. The poet has committed himself to the woman, the physical and not the mythical woman. And the risks are great: "What is it that/ is finally so helpless,/ different, despairs of its own/ statement, wants to/ turn away, endlessly/ to turn away"; "Can I eat/ what you give me. I/ have not earned it"; "Love what do I think/ to say, I cannot say it." Nevertheless, effortlessly, the questions are answered or perhaps simply allowed to dissolve into irrelevancy: "Into the company of love/ it all returns." What appears to be a shallow conclusion is anything but that, because the poet has been through hell and has seen it all.[17]

For Love is then in one small sense at least the archetypal journey from darkness to light. Using an image from several poems in this volume, the poet is the traveler, searching for answers, and finally finding one, at least. This is no odyssey back to home and Penelope, nor a journey through the inferno to paradise, nor a journey into the heart of darkness, though it has miniaturized elements of all and more. Rather, *For Love* probes with intensely personal honesty Creeley's own experiences with love, even to the point of vulnerability. The volume chronicles his own crisis and his coping with it. It has technical precision and control, but more important than that, it deals with a desperately human problem: how to love and how to accept love. *For Love* remains Creeley's most widely read collection.

CHAPTER 5

Fiction

A S it is in Creeley's poetry so it is in his fiction: the word, the fact
of the word, the insistence on the fact of the word. And, above
all, the sufficiency of that fact. No more is needed, and no more is
there. For Creeley a poem is a poem and not a statement about
something else. It is a complex of words, which needs no justification for its existence other than its existence. Its form, its rhythms,
its syntax are true to its own impulses, which are the impulses of the
poet. So too the story, perhaps more so, or at least more clearly so.
A painting of a tree is a painting *of* a tree, but a Jackson Pollock
construct of browns and blacks is autumn rhythms. A Creeley
story—as a Creeley poem—is not *about* anything; it is. And to
"understand" Creeley the reader needs merely to look at his work in
this way.

Warren Tallman, the most perceptive critic of Creeley's fiction,
introduced a collection of recent American short stories by contrasting the writing of this volume with earlier American writing:
"The chief difference, then, between the older American writing
and the new is that writing considered as a means to an end, sentences used as corridors leading to further rooms, and writing considered as an end in itself. The latter will seem limited only to readers
who fail to realize that books contain not persons, places and things
but words"[1] This is not to say that Creeley belongs to a school of
fiction writers any more than he belongs to a school of poets. Seeing
fiction composed of words generating from their own and the writer's individual impulses necessitates uniqueness. One need only
look at the variety of stories collected in *The Gold Diggers* (1965;
expanded from a 1954 collection). Also, while Creeley's fiction is
unique, it is at one with his poetry. The "occasion" of a story is a
moment frozen in time. Things happen, but minimally. We get only
as much as is needed and not one syllable more. And yet it is

enough. Then too, the rhythms are intimate with the impulses of the spoken language, tightening and relaxing syntactically and emotionally. Tallman is right in insisting that these stories must be read aloud.

Most of Creeley's stories were written early in his career, roughly contemporaneous with the composition of the poems in the first half of *For Love*. Briefly, all sixteen stories appear in general order of composition, with nine written between 1948 and 1951, five during 1953 and 1954, and one during 1960.[2] His only novel, *The Island*, was written between September 1960 and January 1963; and although no more novels or short stories have appeared, Creeley has published a long prose piece in *A Day Book* (1972) and *Presences, A Text for Marisol* (1972; discussed in Chapter Six), which are difficult to classify but which could slip over into a sagging definition of fiction.

I   The Gold Diggers

Replying in 1965 to Linda Wagner, Creeley explained the difference as he sees it between poetry and fiction:

Poetry seems to be written momently—that is, it occupies a moment of time. There is, curiously, no time in writing a poem. I seem to be given to work in some intense moment of whatever possibility, and if I manage to gain the articulation necessary *in* that moment, then happily there is a poem. In prose there's a coming and going. Much more of a gathering process is evident in prose writing. In fact I think I undertook prose because it gave me a more extended opportunity to think *in* something—to think around and about and in something which was on my mind.[3]

We have seen how Creeley has been increasingly concerned with fixing the moment in a poem, not so much stopping time as capturing the instance of an emotion so precisely that it occurs between two heartbeats rather than during them, or perhaps resembles a frame of a moving picture. Fiction, however, works in time, both to Creeley's advantage and disadvantage. The advantage is as he explains it: it allows him room to develop and to pursue implications. The disadvantage is that he must relinquish the fixed moment. But saying that, more must be said, because Creeley has written both a novel and short stories and he early realized the differences between them for him. In his preface to the 1954 edition of *The Gold Diggers*, which he retained in the 1965 expanded version, he observed: "Whereas the novel is a continuum, of necessity, chapter to chapter, the story can escape some of that obligation, and function exactly in terms of whatever emotion best can serve it."[4] The short story then—or "tale" as Creeley prefers—allows for greater development and amplification than does the poem, while at the same time it allows for greater concentration and focus than does the novel. Perhaps for these reasons, many readers find Creeley's short stories more satisfying than either his poems or his novel.

A Creeley short story reduces plot to a minimal role; it is there, but barely, serving as a peg upon which to hang the particular emotional complex. It serves little or no structural function, since a Creeley story has none of the Aristotelian necessities—beginning, middle, and end; in fact, he consciously rejected these in his preface, insisting that "the only actuality is life, the only end (never realized) death, and the only value, what love can manage."[5] Neither does Creeley use Freudian-Joycean associational synapses to structure his story. He rejects, too, the carefully calculated non-sequiturs used by many of his contemporaries such as Donald Barthelme to reflect the absurdity or value-bankruptcy of their world. Rather, Creeley arranges words and sentences to produce rhythms and counterrhythms (manipulating—as Tallman insists—syntax rather than sense) that both give form to and are reflections of the emotion that is the occasion for the story.

All this is not to suggest, however, that a Creeley story is devoid of the human; in fact, all his stories are intimately concerned with—as are his novel and most of his poems—human contact or its absence and with an individual's response to that condition. As he said in 1968: "I am given as a man to work with what is most intimate to me—these senses of relationship among people. I think, for myself at least, the world is most evident and most intense in those relationships. Therefore, they are the materials of which my work is made."[6] Intimacy in human relationships and intimacy in human utterance, the emotion produced by the experience and the phrase produced by the breath—working as one, quietly.

In "The Grace," for example, written in 1951 and published that year in *Origin*, the plot is simple: two months after moving to a new house, a husband and wife sit at night in the living room, discussing the house and the move, gradually moving toward lovemaking. When this is interrupted by the crying of their child upstairs, they take a walk through the surrounding fields, settle on the ground, and, again, when about to embrace, hear the child crying. The wife

runs home, quiets the child; the father returns; but the child continues to cry intermittently with briefer moments of quietness. Finally, the father loses his temper, rushes into the child's room,
shouting, and slaps the child's face. Amid the increased screaming,
the father walks beside the bed, cradling his son, helpless, and then
returns to his wife in the other room.

Even in this plot summary, a rhythmical movement plays itself
out from the relatively relaxed beginning to the tense ending; however, even this is too simplified, since tension exists early in the
story with the husband and wife discussing the effects of the move
and with the semiawkward or uncomfortable relationship between
them revealed by his realization of her dislike for the house—"We
can hope for another place, he added. This is just for the time-being.
Call it a vacation, or anything like that" (*Gold Diggers,* 91). The
ending, too, while screwed up to an emotional intensity, concludes
with the husband carrying the child "back to the other room to find
her waiting with the candle" (97). The effect is circular rather than
linear, the action curving away from the house to the fields and then
back to the house. The emotion, the tension from which the husband hopes to escape, is folded back, and the hero is trapped by the
structure of the story.

But this emotion, which is the occasion of the story—this
helplessness, frustration, feeling of entrapment—is made more precise in two additional ways: counterpoint of certain images and
counterpoint of rhythms. First the images, or more precisely, the
image of light. Suffusing the exterior scene and, in varying degrees,
the interior is the moonlight, making objects not just white or bluish
but translucent, making itself felt with a substantial presence,
"pushing to make a space." During the course of the story the moon
rises and falls, but in the middle of the story, when the husband and
wife leave the house to walk in the fields, the moon is there, "very
much a whiteness and lying on the ground with grace" (94). The
ease of the moonlight is grace, but more so is its perfect naturalness;
it occupies its place with its own insistence. It simply *is,* perfectly—much like the father's grandmother, in fact:

But he had started, and spoke, now, of what he had thought himself to
have forgotten, a picnic so long ago it seemed inconsequential, though he
could not have said, then, why. Somewhere his grandmother had carried
out the lemonade, or he remembered it, in a bright tin pitcher, to place it
on the long table, under the trees.

It should be like that, he said. What do we give of that, or what do we try to. Tell me one thing we do that is as nice as that. (92)

Or like the old lady who once lived in their house: "Or that other, the one the old man told us about, his mother, who died by the window there, took three drags on her pipe and then slipped out. How about that!" (93). But certainly not like the father, who is constantly irritated not just by his son's crying, but by a certain disquietude that he cannot explain and perhaps does not understand.

The wife stands in contrast to her husband. Because of the point of view we see only what he sees of her (even her "rigidness" is his interpretation of her movement), and his view is at best ambiguous. She obviously does not understand him and his feelings (he thinks, feeling sorry for himself, although he never admits it); and yet she has a calm, indeed a grace, that he lacks. She can return to the crying child endlessly and not be upset; and it is she to whom he returns after slapping the child in frustrated helplessness. Finally, it is she who carries the candle, not moonlight certainly, but light, at least. The wife's role becomes clear in the last sentence of the story: "But useless, the screaming now louder, and he felt it useless, picking the boy up, to cradle him, holding him, and walking beside the bed's length, the moon still against them, a light, a light, he said, and went back to the other room to find her waiting with the candle" (97). The moon is there; but the husband still calls for a light, and the wife is there. This is no false sentiment or easy solution. The husband is forced to confront the reality, however unsatisfactory, of his present place.

This story, like all Creeley stories, is a rhythmic construct. Even without plot and images, the "point" of the story would be made by Creeley's manipulation of rhythm. This is a simple concept and by no means original, but for Creeley rhythmic movement becomes a dominant factor, the dominant factor in his fiction as it is in his poetry. The critic need only say, "There, listen." The counterpoint between the approaching ease of the husband-wife relationship and the tense intrusion of the child's crying and the counterpoint between the moonlight's easy presence and its later insufficiency are mirrored in the counterpoint between the extended phrasing and natural syntax of the relatively relaxed moments and the short phrases and less natural syntax of the tense moments, and, of course, all gradations in between. A few excerpts illustrate the construction:

Outside it grew light, or seemed to, almost like day, but whiter, again that transluscence, and he wondered if out there one might not be another thing altogether, even though it should seem otherwise. To the west were some small lights, single, each a small brightness, and separate from the rest. He imagined gaiety, or even singing, the tables of some place packed and people altogether without malice. He thought it might be like that, and felt, too, the moon was the sign. (92)

And: "Then she got into the bed, and lay down, coming to him, then, but nothing, he thought, and heard it, the cry, and got up himself to run to the door, pulling at it, and yelled, what, seeing the boy sitting straight in the bed, staring, and crying, screaming, the sound driving in on him as he came" (97).

One might expect the first paragraph to be more relaxed, since reflection is a more relaxed activity than is reacting to a tense situation, but notice how in the second paragraph the phrases are not just shorter but the number of heavily stressed syllables are much more numerous relative to the total: "and yélled, whát, séeing the bóy, sítting stráight in the béd, staring and crýing, scréaming, the sóund dríving in on him as he cáme." This effect is accomplished not just by including more stressed syllables but by reducing the number of unstressed syllables, hence the clipped syntax, and by using present participles that do not need subjects, helping verbs, and the like. Tension—concentrated emotion—is achieved through concentrated language, under pressure, about to blow.

The rhythmic modulations can be seen everywhere in Creeley's prose, most obviously, of course, in contrasting paragraphs such as those above, but these modulations can also be seen when he moves less dramatically along the emotional scale:

Even so, the moon rose, higher, and now came clear through the door they had left open, and came across the floor very softly, to touch the back of his chair. He grew quiet, sinking down, and pushed out his legs, reaching her, one foot against her own.

From somewhere above the boy cried, whimpering, and putting down the knitting, she got up, to cross the stairs, and then he heard her go up, the crying continuing, and growing louder. He started to get up himself, but sat down, annoyed, and wondered what the matter was, calling to her, to hear her answer, nothing. (93).

The phrases of the first paragraph proceed easily, the husband relaxing as the moonlight moves slowly across the room. In the second paragraph, however, the whimpering upsets the scene, not so violently as later, of course, but enough; and the movement becomes more jagged, the phrases more insistent. The wife puts *down* the knitting, gets *up, crosses* the stairs, and the husband starts to get *up* and then sits *down*. In this passage Creeley's use of commas to "score" the movement of the prose can be seen easily. In poetry, the comma's equivalent is the line end.

And these modulations can be observed, felt, throughout the story, providing a pattern of alternate tensing and relaxing, building to the climax when the father strikes the child, a climax that is eased slightly but not resolved in the last long phrase, "and went back to the other room to find her waiting with the candle." The rhythm of that final phrase, in context, is saying that the desperate feeling of being trapped has eased somewhat but certainly has not disappeared. The man has taken one step back from the verge, but both he and the verge remain, one step apart.

Any discussion of Creeley's subtle rhythms must oversimplify, but the point is clear, and it is more than that form and content work together. Rather, it is—as in his poems—that form becomes content. Rhythm is not used to underscore what plot and image are doing; plot and image are used to underscore rhythm, and Creeley's rhythm comes close to capturing that emotion that words such as "frustration" or "entrapment" can only suggest.

Each Creeley story is different, with a unique rhythmic pattern flowing from the emotion that was and is the instance and insistence of the story and the man. For example, Creeley's earliest story, "The Unsuccessful Husband," describes a dismal marriage as told by the husband shortly after his wife's funeral. He was—as he remains—temperamentally incapable of caring, even reacting; hence the rhythm is more consistent, laconic but not relaxed, plodding on, and the contrast to the emotions that the husband should be feeling is captured perfectly in the story's final paragraph:

The next day I have already spoken of, such a calm and peaceful day, and I spent the greater part of it arranging for her funeral. Needless to say, I had only to express a few brief wishes and the rest of the matter was taken out of my hands. The day of her funeral passed without event and I found myself watching her go into the ground without much feeling of any kind. I knew

that her part in it was over and my own very nearly so. In any event it was
something to think about. (19)

At the rhythmic extreme from "The Unsuccessful Husband" is the
first of "Three Fate Tales." The narrator here is lonely, observing
normal daily activities: "The little girl has a ball. It bounces on the
floor. Its noise is exact. The woman calls her for her dinner, she
complains, doesn't want to come" (46). And observing abnormal
activities, such as the child falling from the window: "Nothing of the
woman until her head is just opposite mine, the mouth wide,
scream, and someone I see the face of below, looks up and calls to
her. It's all right. She isn't hurt. A miracle" (47). All with deadening
sameness. But this man is inwardly torn by his loneliness and his
isolation from others, making self-identification impossible, a tor-
ture that comes out as the muted scream of the first paragraph: "I
put it this way. That I am, say, myself, that this, or this feel, you
can't have, or from that man or this, me, you can't take it. And what
I would do, with any of this, is beyond you, and mine. But for this
time, yours too" (45). This paragraph, which several reviewers
quoted as unintelligible, demonstrates why the Creeley reader
should concentrate on syntax, because it is precisely the broken
syntax that conveys the broken probing of the narrator.

Creeley's final story in *The Gold Diggers*, "The Book," written
more than a decade after "The Unsuccessful Husband" and at the
time of the early poems of *Words*, retains the markings of all
Creeley stories. It tells of a man, drunk, who is making a bumbling
attempt at reconciliation with a woman who has left him. Again, the
end returning to the beginning is there. The first sentence: "He was
bringing the book in a gesture of final hope" (153), and the ending:
"Get the book to her. Get the goddamn book to her. Show her what
you can do. The book with the songs" (158). A doomed and desperate attempt, struggling and failing, but somehow eliciting admiration more than pity—not heroic failure certainly, but almost heroic
attempt. At least he keeps trying, even if it is the alcohol that pushes
him, that somehow makes sense out of a senseless situation. The flat
rhythms are here also and the broken syntax reflecting the man's
drunken semiconfusion, but something more. This story contains
the overt insistence on the reality of the thing, the object, that we
have seen in *Words:* "You're not listening. Yes but he couldn't get
the words. Like this, and one, and two, like this, and, there, you

hear it, now, and one, and two" (158). The groping desperation of
the halting, flailing rhythms suggest the man's desperate, doomed
gamble.

And, finally, one must see this story moving, more than his earlier
stories, toward a statement about poets and poetry, again consistent
with some of his concerns in *Words*. The book of songs, of course, is
the writer's gift to a too often disinterested world, but this sentimen-
tal notion is saved by having the writer portrayed in an unattractive
light, in effect deserving the treatment, almost: "He wasn't that
drunk. He was heartbroken. He was hot, tired with walking, wanted
to drink beer, wanted friends, a home, wife and friends and beer.
He sang a song for that sound. He kept walking but it wasn't fair any
more"; to which Creeley adds finally, "You're not listening" (158).
All through the story, parallels are insisted upon between the man
trying to give his book to the woman and the poet reaching outside
himself to an audience.

This discussion has throughout insisted upon the rhythmic
uniqueness of each story, but what of the unity of the volume itself?
In a sense, the observation that each story makes use of rhythm as
more than a literary device, indeed as a physical response to an
emotion, helps to demonstrate a consistency among them. Beyond
this, however, most commentators on these stories have observed
the obvious: all Creeley's stories explore relationships, usually broken, unfulfilled, or unsatisfying, that exist between people, precisely the material of the first two-thirds of *For Love*. Reviewer
Anthony Keller said in *Commonweal*: "Almost without exception
the characters of *The Gold Diggers* are victims of a profound loneliness for which companionship provides only a tenuous remedy.
Emanating from a reducing mirror, they are depicted in varying
postures of repression, escape and despair. There are no heroes; just
people getting along."[7] And Samuel Moon in *Poetry* adds, "The
subject of the stories is that kind of relation between people which is
penetration, a locking or growing together in which the life becomes
not what each one has alone but what is between them—all the
inseparable pains and pleasure, terror and joys of that kind of relation, in its presence, or at times its absence."[8] Certainly, this is the
recurrent theme of *The Gold Diggers* (although as Creeley has said
his "point" is that he is writing), and it helps give this volume a unity
of impact. It may help, however, to think of these relationships not
so much as theme—final statement—but as instances that produce

the particular emotions of the stories, emotions that can be described in no other way than the story itself. Nevertheless, relationships, usually marital, which fail in one way or another, are present in all stories, as observed in the stories discussed so far and as easily seen in the others. The opening paragraph of "The Dress" describes a typical couple:

> Much was simple about Mary and Peter, and to describe them quickly, it was first of all two people, in a house into which not many others came. And three children, pushed into corners, and a friend or two who came to call. After ten years or so of living together, there were no very actual mementos, or none that either felt much disposition to recognise. There were no flags, and in fact few signs of even time except for the children, and a scar which traversed Mary from belly-button to bottom. Which both had *done*, but also for which Peter was in some sense guilty. Not her. (145)

Elsewhere, "The Musicians" presents a situation of unfulfilling homosexual love; "The Lover" describes a man, guilt-ridden and strangely dissatisfied, who thinks of how much he dislikes his wife, even in the midst of sex; and "The Boat" presents several kinds of incomplete relationships. The wife is presently deceiving her husband and decides to leave him for a man she does not seem to like. The children attempt, almost successfully, to kill their father by running him down with their boat. All characters remain fixed to the others but, simultaneously, trapped within themselves, a condition suggested most obviously by the woman:

> Looking past them, she saw a briefcase, on the seat of a chair, with gold initials just over the lock. She went over and picked it up, and tried to open it, but could not, and threw it back in the chair in anger. It was the life of a dead man, not to have kindness, and openness, in each person met or dealt with. To have secrets was finally to have desires, and if she could not satisfy them, to keep them like that was dishonest. She picked up the briefcase again and threw it into a bed of yellow flowers. What she gave was open, and all air, she thought. But for them it was the careful locking up of each particular, because they thought they were men. (114)

A locked briefcase: a perfect image of how people see people in a Creeley story.

One final point must be made concerning the interrelationships of the stories in *The Gold Diggers*. Warren Tallman in his essay, "Robert Creeley's Rimethought," notes Creeley's repetition of similar though not identical objects: "In one story children play with sticks and throw stones. The sticks rime into twigs, bark, branches, boats, tables, chairs, houses, trees, and the stones rime into pebbles, rocks, boulders, a gravestone, and chunks of gold searched for as in an alchemist's dream."[9] This process, a kind of topological progression, is far more dense, Tallman suggests, than any simple pattern or cluster of images might be. In fact, it accounts for the extreme specificity of the words themselves. Tallman then goes on to discuss, legitimately, this process as it occurs in *For Love*.

But not all commentators on *The Gold Diggers* have been so complimentary; some have been critical of Creeley's style, others of his tone, and still others have simply been admittedly confused. Bernard Bergonzi put it metaphorically: "It's rather like trying to tune in a talk on a remote radio station, with interference and static drowning a large part of what is being said."[10] Saul Maloff expressed another common reservation: "The principal limitation . . . resides in the oneness of tone, the small range of theme, subject, and feeling—so that all the stories seem fragments of a single mosaic."[11] And an English reviewer, D. J. Enright, coupled an attack on Creeley with an attack on avant garde writing generally—that is, writing that reduces subject matter and avoids significant statement. "The reaction [of fiction such as Creeley's] is against the fat juicy novel."[12]

Then too, many reviewers compared *The Gold Diggers* to Creeley's novel, *The Island*, which had been published two years earlier, in 1963, even though all the stories of *The Gold Diggers* had been written and originally published before *The Island*. Indeed, it was the novel's success that had caused Scribner's to publish the commercial edition of the stories. While other reviewers noted obvious thematic and plot similarities between the two works, Samuel Moon emphasized the difference in terms of focus and intensity, with the stories located somewhere between the novel and the poetry: "The stories are comparable in length to the chapters of the novel, but their intensity is much greater. The poems are at the other end of the range, straining articualtion to its limits and approaching absolute intensity."[13] Certainly, the stories are less intense than many of the poems; length alone would dictate this; however, the stories are short enough to allow Creeley that momentary complex of emotions that he desired to make real. His novel, because of its greater length and because it is a "continuum," can not quite freeze the moment.

II   The Island

The Island was begun September 7, 1960, while Creeley was tutoring in Guatemala, with approximately the first quarter of the novel written within that month and most of the second part written during January of 1962 while Creeley was teaching English at the University of New Mexico. The third and fourth sections were written during the fall and winter of 1962–1963 while Creeley was teaching at the University of British Columbia.[14] These are the dates of composition, but the events upon which the novel is based occur much earlier. In May 1951, the Creeleys moved to Fontrousse, near Aix-en-Provence in southern France, where they lived until May 1952, when they moved to nearby Lambesc. At the urging of Martin Seymour-Smith, a young English writer who was tutoring Robert Graves' son on Mallorca, the Creeleys moved to the Spanish Island known to some extent as an expatriate writers' colony. The Creeleys lived in Banyalbufour until October 1954, and then in Bouanova until July 1955, when Creeley returned to Black Mountain College and ended his marriage of nine years. *The Island* draws in considerable detail on Creeley's experiences during these years, with most of the plot taken from 1953. Ostensibly, the novel describes the growing strain of the Creeley marriage and the struggle within Creeley over his proper role as an artist, but of course it involves much more than that. The events, as one might expect of Creeley, are ordinary, understated, and numerous. Much happens, and most of it trivial, which is of course the point.

The story opens with Artie visiting John and Joan after a late night drunken session. Artie's intrusion into John and Joan's night simply prepares for the continuing and widening division between them that is a large part of the novel; and Artie's insistence that John return to his house with him prepares us for that love-hate relationship. The trio sets up the central conflict within John: on the one hand is the pull and repulsion of his craft as a writer (Artie-art) and on the other is the pull and repulsion of the ordinary world (Joan-domesticity). As in one section of *For Love*, containing poems written during and immediately following the breakup of his marriage (approximately the same time period of the novel), the muse demands total obedience, an obedience that John, because of his circumstances and temperament, cannot give. And, as these circumstances work themselves out—or more precisely wind themselves down—John and Artie go drinking, friends and strangers visit, John and his family go on picnics, various people go swimming, Artie buys a radio, John buys a boat, and John frequently thinks back over his past, continually analyzing his motives and his attitudes. Two events, however, clearly stand out as pivotal and climactic, coming as they do in the precise middle and end of the novel. At the end of Part Two, Joan nearly dies from a broken cyst, her body filling with pus; thereafter, she is not the same, nor is the relationship. And, at the novel's close, John, believing Joan has fallen from a cliff into the sea, undergoes a complete emotional catharsis, feeling real emotion, grief, for the first time in years, only to return to their house to find Joan alive and unaware of what he has experienced.

The examination of the main character is painfully precise. As in the poems of this period and the stories, Creeley, the narrator, narrows the traditional gap between narrator and protagonist, baring with total honesty the protagonist's—and Creeley's—pettiness, impotency, and anguish. It is tempting, and to some extent would be justified, to say that the novel examines the predicament of the artist in this domesticated world; however, it is truer and certainly more complete to say that John is both more than the artist and less. He is a vulnerable, self-pitying, often unpleasant, often confused man; and yet he is attractive, largely because while he plays games with others, he tries to be honest with himself. In short, he appears to others the way most of us do and appears to himself the way we appear to ourselves. The value of the novel, then, lies in the humanity of John's character and with the fidelity to human relationships examined here.

The novel contains many conflicts—of relationships, obviously, but of other sorts as well—and they constantly shift, the parts rarely fitting. The island itself is a place to which one escapes, but it is also, alternately, insistent isolation. The sea is warm, wet, fecund, and also distant, aloof. Each character is part of the "mismatched pattern" of the book, yet each is supremely alone, touching others as two people going into the sea in diving suits, "going down into the water together, touching through the suits and that subtle medium, speaking through tubes and wires." Even this artificially maintained relationship continues only because proper distancing devices are regulated with restraint. "In the sea the bodies rise and fall, but slowly, with careful regard for pressure. In the suits which cover them there is opportunity to adjust to the changes of pressure. Of this regard or of that, of this or that insistence. With care it can be controlled. The body will not be allowed to explode. It will rise or fall at the gradual pace of the will, the term of the communication."[15]

But as much as the book is *about* the difficulty of relationships, the book *is* a book of awkwardness—stumbling, twisted, ugly, incompetent, and above all else, terribly human awkwardness. In Warren Tallman's phrase, the primary rimethought is awkwardness; it is a dominant motif, which occurs and recurs in form after form on practically every page of the novel. It underlines the rapidly deteriorating relationship between John and Joan; it points up the art-domesticity conflict within John; it supports, in fact largely produces, the tone of ironic hopelessness and despair that permeates the novel; and it finally manifests itself in the often difficult syntax and rhythms of the sentences. Either the characters fail to drop into the "whimsical plan of it all" and they usually do fail, the pattern remaining fragmented, incomplete; or they fall numbed into a pattern that makes impossible authentic feeling: "They dumbly followed a pattern" (123). In either case, life is not lived with ease and naturalness. The parts simply do not fit, and every act, every thought rubs raw these relationships.

The awkward motif recurs often, remaining as a constant presence and taking many forms. For instance, early in the novel, the narrator describes a father and "a crippled son, a bird-like boy, favoring the twisted leg" (25), on the beach, shunned by the other bathers; and then he immediately describes the baron who once had lived there and who often swam alone on these shores, watched by a few of the curious who "crawled out on the over-hanging bluffs to see his stilted, thin figure move stiffly into the water" (25). Several pages later John describes his own view—"with a clearing head"—of Artie: he "seemed to become a fumbling, disjointed poor fellow" (28). And then John, still under the influence of some pills he and Artie had taken, decides to buy a painting of a dead bullfighter described by the narrator as "awkward, lumpish" (29). Later the bullfighter's face is said to have an "incompetent deadness" (36), which John tries to

pass off as "grotesque incompetence" (37). "Couldn't they laugh
about it?" he asks of Joan, who sees his foolishness (as she always
does), "make of it a gentle joke, a soft, fumbling reminder of mortal-
ity?" (37). And so it goes. John buys a worthless painting, while Joan
falls in love with Rene, a painter-friend who is a perfect example of
the self-assured competent craftsman. Everywhere, directly or indi-
rectly, by example and by suggestion is the evidence of John's
stumbling, fumbling incompetency. Even in the climax of the
novel's first half John fails to measure up. In a "cluttered" restau-
rant, Joan suddenly becomes seriously ill with an internal broken
cyst. She is physically twisted with pain, the "tears slipping down
her tightened face" (93), and he carries her first to one clinic, which
gives no help and indeed appears to misapprehend the situation,
and then to another, rushing in, terrified, "stumbling with Joan's
weight" (93). The broken cyst of course suggests the end of their
marriage, the poisonous pus flooding her intestines and nearly kill-
ing her; however, the denouement is worked out through the second half of the book. Joan has changed permanently, and John
becomes even less capable of coping with their relationship.

The awkward motif continues through the second half of the novel
with even more direct references to John's incompetencies. "He
fumbled in a distance of his own" (133); "He drank with a persistent,
awkward care, afraid he might spill everything all over the table or
on the people crowded at other tables all around him" (155);
"Nothing John tried to cover things with could manage" (164). Even
sex is difficult to manage with ease. While making love, Joan falls
asleep, causing John to remember their first attempt. At her insistence, "he tried to, fumbling, because he didn't know clearly where
even he might, or how to, till the excitement brought him hard
against her but not in, and he spurted in a trembling incompetence
all over her legs" (171–72). Other episodes persistently underscore
this motif, all building toward the second major climax and final
embarrassment for John. Following a violent argument, Joan runs
out of the house and does not return. John, becoming increasingly
concerned, begins to search for her in the darkness, finally convincing himself that she has fallen from the cliffs to her death.
Distraught, weeping, he returns to waken the children and tell
them of the tragedy. The novel's conclusion is a master stroke of
understated irony:

He tried to say, your mother, but they were too close to him and he couldn't say it. He looked and in a sudden, blurred instant she was there, holding Jennie, looking down at them, asking incredibly with everything as it had been, what is it, John. What's the matter.

He pulled clear of the two boys, got up, and stood, looking at her face, and began to put out his hand, toward her, then stopped. I thought you were dead, he said, but I was wrong. (189–90)

And irony upon irony. He was not wrong. She was dead, in at least several senses of that word. First, she was dead symbolically; their relationship was finally ended. And, second, she was dead to John. Her presence had been a constant reminder of his own incompetencies. She was capable; he was not: "As she undressed, he took off his own clothing, awkward, a little embarrassed" (65). He had trouble communicating easily with people in another language and another culture: "Joan spoke the language more easily, feeling easier to begin with. She became intimate with the town's people" (40). Now that was ended. The possible ambiguity of the conclusion (was he really free since she still quite literally lives?) is dismissed when one remembers that during his grief at what he assumed was his wife's death, he let his feelings flow easily for the first time in the novel. He wept, he admitted his hatred for her, and, finally, he returned from the cliffs freely, surely. "He had come as she had made him, stumbling out into the vagueness, crawling after her" (189); but now, "he felt calmer, the air was cool and fresh. He began to walk back toward the house but slowly because he had still to think of how to recover her most simply" (189). His sureness is defined most graphically in the moments before he discovered his wife is still alive:

He was crying. Nothing could hold it back, and he felt it coming through him for all the years and years of his impotence and guilt, and the self-hate that wouldn't let go when it had to, but waited until it had killed itself and everything around it. His children, himself. He knelt down to them, they were looking at him, confused, one saying something he could not hear distinctly, but he took them, reached out for both, and pulled them, crying, into his arms. (189)

His release is secured at the novel's end, but if one looks back over the novel, it becomes clear that alternate release or at least its possibility had always been there. The sea provided it. "He walked into the water, ducked, and began to swim out, relaxing" (70); and

"It was always a pleasure, and diving in, John swam clear of the sloshing kelp and headed out" (83). Those moments he spent bobbing in his small, confessedly ugly sailboat provided it. In fact, he was drawn to this boat because it seemed as incongruous here as he did, "its inappropriate place there among all the ease and rightness of the glib, sure fleet of the richly confident" (126). But most of all, the potential release was there in his writing, even though he was writing little, restricted as he was by his life on the island:

> What to say, then. Pinched by the sight, he began to write as he was able, small, twisted sketches of things, stories of a kind, distortions, fragments of acts that got displaced by the words as he worked to test the meanings, the signs. There was occasion enough to hold him, but what happened to the possibility, say, or did it all have to mean what he meant by it. There were endless positions, endless grinning heads, endless places all were to be in, but then they slipped past to others, sat where he had never wanted them to, slippery, undefined. He thought that if he were able to begin with his own head, detach that in some way, make it a possibility also, loose and free, so that he could see the back of it for example, and surprise it by terms it would not yield to him if only some projection of his neck, a growth, a thing that went with him, all of a piece. . . ." (116)

Ironically, of course, the passage describes Creeley's own work of this period quite accurately, but in this context he apparently intends this description as a serious qualification of his writing.[16] Later in the novel he turns down a willing publisher of his stories, regretting his decision shortly thereafter. Clearly, Creeley is saying that competency, in art as in life, is not possible within the conditions of this novel. The conditions must change for John and his art to be released. And what are those conditions? On the level of life, they are the fragmented, incomplete, suspicious, witholding relationships of the novel, particularly of course between John and Joan (those common, interchangeable names); on the level of art they are in Robert Graves' term simple domesticities.

As in his poetry of this period, we return to the inevitable conflict within the artist between his art, that is, his muse, and the domestic life. The White Goddess demands complete allegiance; other women, such as wives, make such allegiance impossible. Creeley's novel, however, is not simply a working out of Graves' White Goddess thesis (even though Graves is by Creeley's own admission the model for Duddon, the poet of the island and Artie's employer);

rather, Creeley used the myth of the goddess to underline the conflict in the novel between the artist's needs for uninhibited release of authentic feeling and the terribly restricted confinement of this artist's life. Although no one woman represents the White Goddess, various women, even Joan at times, suggest release for John. Artie's wife, Marge, remains aloof from John, even it seems from Artie. In a world of herself, helped with tranquilizers, unable to cope with everyday necessities, and yet able to see through the little games that John and Artie play, she at least momentarily seems to offer John escape from domesticity. After leaving Artie off at the writer's house early in the novel, John returns to Marge, but first stops off in a bar where he watches "the large ripe pleasure" of a girl's breasts as she bends over a bicycle. Upon seeing Marge shortly after, he transfers "the bar girl's breasts to her own long chest, and the image broke, leaving her sitting comfortably across from him at the table with her cup of coffee" (21). Domesticity triumphs. An even more improbable release for John is in the unattractive sister of an Australian writer who came to live for a short time on the island. She is "grotesquely cheerful" and appeals to John with her enthusiasm and her flaunting of custom; however, she must leave the island after swimming nude within sight of a fisherman, thus breaching local mores.

But, finally, it is Joan herself who becomes briefly a manifestation of the muse. Shortly after moving into La Baronia, John takes his family for a picnic on a hill above the town. They eat, the children wander off, and he tells her he loves her. Here, above the town, beside a spring that may have gone back to the Greeks, Joan is transformed. She puts a crown of flowers on her head and becomes "an image of the goddess" (42). "Aren't you happy, she said. Isn't it a lovely place" (42). But, of course, it could not last. "The small woman had just performed a ritual. I love you, he said. A clutter" (43). And it was all over, even though the final destruction does not occur until Joan is near death from the broken cyst. As John drives back from the hospital that night, he looks out at the moon and at the moon's image in the sea, where "he saw a shattered white face blurred with shifting water, a painful thing" (94). The shattered white face is Joan's, but it is also the moon, symbol of the goddess. Here the reality of a destroyed relationship and the theme of art versus domesticity meet in the image of the shattered moon.

Again, not to overstate the point, the novel is not about the

White Goddess; it is a picture of awkwardness. Various forms of the goddess, the sea itself, indeed embattled art provide release from this sense of not fitting, but the novel's point is that things do not fit, at least not easily, at least not for John. And yet John remains in some ways attractive. He is a victim of modern domestic life, but he knows this and examines his relationship to this life with often embarrassing honesty. He constantly fumbles but always turns in to look at himself, and what he finds there is a terribly human individual. Technically, the distance between the narrator and John disappears, and so too does the distance between the narrator and the reader. For the duration of the novel, and perhaps beyond, we become John.

Only one other point needs to be made, and it is an obvious point. Just as awkwardness remains the dominant motif of the novel so, too, does it dictate the novel's syntax and rhythms. As in the short stories and the poems, rhythms are modulated through manipulation of syntax in order to demonstrate the kind of impulse giving rise to the line; and again, every page is replete with examples. The novel, however, contains a much greater range of rhythms than do the short stories, determined perhaps by the greater need for shifting pace in a longer form and by the impossibility of maintaining over many pages the kind of intensity a story of just several pages can sustain. The brief stacatto units are there at painful moments as when John tries, unsuccessfully of course, to inject Joan with some medicine following her stay in the hospital: "What could he do. He had to, clearly. There was to be no running, no explanations. There was nothing at all to talk about. It was a very simple thing to do. He lifted his hand, then swung it down, at the pinch of flesh, felt the needle seem to bend, stop, and saw the scratch, by his hand, across her skin. She jerked and pushed up with her hands" (99). But the novel also contains, though far fewer, relaxed passages as when John has mastered to some degree the small boat he has purchased:

He had taken Joan and the children for rides, for picnics on the rocks beyond the beach, holding the boat steady while one after another carefully got out of it, and then, later, in again. He had let them try the oars, pull as he did with an increasing confidence, heading the boat about, or in, or out, or along the edge of the sea. By himself at times he would slip the oars under the decked-over bow, take off his shirt, then flop off into the water to swim beside the bobbing white boat, pushing it ahead of him, lazily, then grab hold and up and in again, and then back to the beach. (131)

And here is the point: that Creeley underlines John's awkwardness with awkward lines and then releases the lines when John manages a bit of competency. His short stories often insist that the point is the rhythm itself; plot, image, even theme are used to support the rhythm that is the story's prime conveyor of feeling. In the novel, however, except in certain brief, tense moments, the rhythms return to their more traditional function, supporting meaning.

This final observation points up an important failure in Creeley's novel, one that makes ultimately unsatisfactory what is certainly an impressive tour de force. The novel succeeds only to a point, failing finally exactly where the poetry and short stories succeed—as form. As mentioned early in this chapter, Creeley is aware of the intense moment possible in the short story and of the novel as a continuum. The short stories and poems succeed because they can isolate an instance of feeling, stop time as it were, and probe with scalpel the dim recesses of a human emotion. The novel, however, simply because of its length, must push ahead; and Creeley's novel does push ahead. Individual scenes, even chapters, are brilliantly conceived but seem to sit there with nowhere to go. At one time Creeley seems to intend a linking of experiences and flashbacks associationally. He thinks of his great-grandfather's ease when dealing with a sly Indian while he himself has stumbled once more. At another time, he seems to link through repetitive motifs, as mentioned earlier. He remembers his difficulty at obtaining luggage in Marseilles and other instances of awkwardness surround him. At still other times, his plot creakily moves the novel along, a plot considerably stronger than any found in his short stories. On the level of plot, just what is his obsession with the boat about anyway? Or Manus and his offer to publish John's stories for that matter? Or the middle-aged woman who wants her poems published? Or Marge's baby? The problem here is not that Creeley links these events thematically, but that he stays within the tradition of the novel to do it. The impulse is to stop each of these moments, but the novel form insists that they go on. Ironically, form, which itself conveys most of what Creeley has to say in his short stories and poems, fails him here. He cannot have both. He can use Joyce's stream of consciousness to link these epiphanic moments. He can use the pronounced surrealism of more contemporary writers. Or he can return to the well-made novel. Or, and this is where he seems to be going, he can search out new and more compatible vehicles for his longer prose. *The Island,* however, impressive though it is, fails to contain itself, easily, completely.

III   A Day Book

Creeley's most recent longer prose extends his search for more compatible vehicles. *A Day Book* insists on its journal characteristics by imprinting "Tuesday, November 19, 1968" on the front cover and "Friday, June 11, 1971" on the back cover. Presumably, the reader is to accept this work as a series of journal entries, although the text runs continuously without individual daily entries identified. Creeley is clearly experimenting with a form that will give some external skeletal shape to his thoughts without necessarily imposing the restrictions of a convention. The journal allows him to roam but, more importantly, it allows him to express directly his thoughts and reactions, a crucial factor for this most intimate of poets. He can speak to us under the pretext of speaking to himself.

A Day Book, as the name itself implies, returns to a constant Creeley preoccupation: the trap of time and the attempt—any success is momentary—to escape the inexorable movement of one moment after another. Near the end of *A Day Book*, when thinking of his Aunt Bernice's imminent death and his mother's resignation that she is next, he lashes out at "that damn history again, the chronological"[17] reflecting a more oblique reference earlier in the work to experience: "It is all somewhat too linear as if thinking were, he thinks, a line to be followed. Another day will be that one. This one, the new morning of a day" (4). But that is just the beginning— time as a trap from which we must escape but cannot—for the implications ripple out from that awareness. The central dilemma is one upon which all art depends. As seen in his other work, especially *Pieces*, freezing the moment in art is a successful, though again temporary, escape from time, but, simultaneously, such an escape depends totally upon the particularity of that moment, which of course gains its particularity through its intimacy with life—in time. The dilemma cannot be solved; it can only be used.

The poem, the story, or any work of art for that matter, can be seen as a moment then, a field upon which the artist works, not linearly, this leading to that, but simultaneously, this and that and that and that. In recalling a dream about John Altoon, a painter and friend now dead, Creeley described his understanding of Altoon's method. First, Altoon's words about a particular painting: "And one

with various trees, one, in particular, dead center, he points to and
says, *that's sincerity*—which I take as meaning, that's as much tree
as was possible to realize, there, that's all of it, all at once, all I see.
And it is—i.e., is crazily intensive seeing, and all *at once*" (61–62).
Creeley then adds his own understanding of Altoon's method:"I see
why paint was always (or in some ways) hang-up for him, too slow for
what he was doing. As times in Mallorca he was mixing pigments as
he worked, finally just dumping turpentine on piles of dry pigment,
not even looking so intent he was on the canvas" (62). The notion
returns us naturally to Olson's "Composition by Field" of twenty
years before, still a vital force for Creeley.

Then too, *A Day Book* records Creeley's attempts to particularize
a moment by using words to capture things, and much of this work is
his response to the immediacy of his physical environment, an intense response recorded in immediate language, almost as though
he were experimenting with how immediate language can be. In
one sense, this concern is revealed in the probing hesitations,
switches of words and thoughts used to get at what he wants to say
but cannot exactly. At one point, for instance, he attempts to describe his aunt when she was young: "The care she took with herself,
in that sense—despite the awkwardness of the colostomy, for her of
all people—her, not daintiness, but very literal femininity. Her
impatience, with either self-indulgent sentiment or any attempt to
get round some actual state of feeling. Sneer, she would—very
truly. Tough—yet respectful, somehow, of actual innocence in men,
that tender state—" (59). This is the exploratory probing of the
surgeon-poet that we have seen in Creeley's other work; however,
in another sense, this concern for immediacy of response is revealed
in frontal attacks, direct unequivocable descriptions of intense
physical experiences, particularly relating to sex. Early in the work
he lamented the decreasing power of words that, previously taboo,
have now lost their power through overuse: "Say anything, i.e.,
shit, fuck, cunt, etc. In my own head these words are now so much a
faded condition, in themselves, no energy seems to come from
them" (14). Shortly afterward, however, Creeley brought those
words, and sexuality itself, to an intensity of erotic climax by describing simply and directly variations of the sex act, responding to
the statement, "It was inextricably time to know a fact" (24). Intercourse, fellatio, cunnilingus, sex involving three and four people, all
described openly, honestly, and powerfully. "Simplify, simplify," a

fellow New Englander of a century previous advised, but it is unlikely he had this in mind.

A Day Book is much more than such simple statement, however, and will be better understood within the context of Creeley's future writing.[18] The journal itself is a conventionalized form, but it is a form that allows the infinite variations and subtleties of rhythm, tone, and texture that characterize both Creeley's prose and poetry. Furthermore, it allows the direct recording of Creeley's intimate involvement with life. And yet it is somehow not totally satisfying, perhaps because Creeley needs the tension produced by working with and against a convention, but perhaps also because he never relaxes into the journal as a journal. His record there remains somewhat studied, consciously a literary product to be read by outsiders. Perhaps he should keep his journal to himself, but that's another dilemma.

CHAPTER 6

Form As Fact

THE tradition within which Creeley writes—the Williams, Olson, Projectivist tradition—insists that the poet be free to choose the form most suitable to the point being made; indeed, as seen in Chapter 2, Creeley maintains that the poem itself must be free to receive the form resulting from its own insistence. Since each utterance is unique, the syllables and lines must arrange themselves into a unique configuration. One observer of Creeley's poems, Robert F. Kaufman, has said flatly: "In fact, the whole idea of formal organization and measure is repugnant to him. . . ."[1] On the other hand, an equally perceptive observer, Carl Harrison-Ford, introduced Creeley to Australian readers by saying that Creeley is "a man who sees recurring patterns. . . ."[2] Both quotations are taken out of context, of course, but they do illustrate the nature of the debate—and for many the confusion—over the shape of Creeley's poetry and fiction. Is it possible to have in poetry both form and flux? Can one man see recurring patterns and yet reject the whole idea of formal organization? Williams is a poet closely associated in the mind of the reading public with "free verse," and yet he came near the end of his career to the "triadic line," a versatile variation of the terza rima, although still a formal construct; and Creeley is a poet whose best known statement may well be, "Form is never more than an extension of content,"[3] and yet his poems consistently arrange themselves in two, three, or four line stanzas, and his fiction, as seen in Chapter 5, exhibits a concern for form and recurring pattern. Any commentator on Creeley's work must decide for himself to what degree Creeley inclines to the formal, to the recurring and stable shape behind a poem or piece of fiction. Is Creeley repelled by formal organization, and if so, how to account for his quatrains? Does he see recurring patterns, and if so, how to account for the bits and fragments particularly of his later poems and for the difficulty of knowing how to read *A Day Book* and *Presences?* Or perhaps form is used by Creeley in the way he saw Whitman's form, while sitting beside the ocean in California: "The constantly recurring structures in Whitman's writing, the insistently parallel sound and rhythms, recall the patterns of waves as I now see them daily."[4] The shape of the wave is always the same, but each wave is unique in its own composition.

I   *Creeley as Classicist*

Again to begin simply: Creeley must be seen as a classicist who needs and in fact uses standard, a priori poetic forms and who more recently has been searching for usable external forms for his poetry, and yet who because of his time, his associations, and his own statements is best known among his contemporaries as a Projectivist poet. The irony upon which he relies so heavily in his poetry and fiction has its parallel here. Perhaps the tentative, probing, hovering rapier technique and the thematic concern with the search for but never attainment of form and self demand a substantial, external form. Whatever the cause, Creeley's poetry exhibits a much greater regularity and formalization than is usually assumed; and, what is even more significant, much of his poetry and prose, especially from the later years, can be understood best as products of the push toward form, of the classical need for preexistent form despite the modernist dismissal of it.

Creeley speaks often of the poem shaping itself while it is being formulated, of the poem assuming its own unique presence resulting from the pressures of the creative circumstance. In this sense, the poet cannot be consciously aware of the form of the poem until the words begin to appear, and for Creeley this apparently means before they begin to appear on the page. In a lecture delivered at the Literarisches Colloquium, Berlin, in 1967, he said. "What I have written I knew little of until I had written it, "[5] echoing a statement made three years earlier, "I have never explicitly known—before writing—what it was that I would say."[6] But—and here is the crucial point—a poem created without conscious preplanning need not be formless. Another New Englander, Robert Frost, user of the stanza and the iamb, claimed for the poem: "It must be a revelation, or a series of revelations, as much for the poet as for the reader."[7]

Creeley too recognizes that a mind can—and must—intuitively

shape the poem that is being uttered, and can—and with Creeley almost always does—fall back upon certain recurrent forms for the outline or at least the skeleton of that shape. In an interview for the *Times Literary Supplement* in 1964, Creeley quoted E. R. Dodds' *The Greeks and the Irrational:* "Automatic or inspirational speech tends everywhere to fall into metrical patterns"[8] and then, two years later, he stated more explicitly what these patterns tend to be for him: "Because I am the man I am, and think in the patterns I do, I tend to posit intuitively a balance of *four*, a foursquare circumstance, be it walls of a room or legs of a table, that reassures me in the movement otherwise to be dealt with."[9] More recently, looking back on nearly three decades of productivity, Creeley acknowledged his predisposition toward patterns. "My tidinesses," he said, "are insistent. Thus the forms of things said moved through accumulated habits of order. . . ."[10] While asserting then, as seen in Chapter 2, that each poem must be true to its own insistence, Creeley quite clearly recognized at least by the midsixties that his poems tend to arrange themselves in certain recurrent patterns, reflecting order, balance, and symmetry. Furthermore, it is possible to follow the interplay between the projective line and rhythm (breath and syllable) and the persistence of pattern throughout the development of Creeley's poetry. Creeley's best poetry, then, does not so much reflect a conflict between Projective Verse and standard forms as a successful fusion of the two.

II   *The Earlier Poetry*

In *For Love*, Creeley's first substantial volume, which covers the formative decade of the 1950s, we can see the poet working out an accommodation between the freedom resulting from his reaction against the fixed metrics of the 1940s and his own predisposition toward pattern. In the early poems such as "Hart Crane," "The Song," "The Crisis," and "Le Fou," Creeley spreads his lines across the page, arranging them in projectivist units. But even here, the pattern hovers in the background, as in "Le Fou." The "organic" quality of this poem has been discussed earlier; it is sufficient here to point out that the poem is based on a 4–2–4 line stanza arrangement once the lines set off from the lefthand margin are either raised to complete the preceding line or are brought back to the lefthand margin. The only exception is the final "goodbye," appropriately so. Such a rearrangement of the line, of course, destroys the

poem—image, rhythm, and line are no longer working together—
but it does reveal a more traditional pattern behind what appears to
be projectivist lining.

Very early, however, Creeley shifted to more overt traditional
stanza forms, usually composed of two or three units with an occasional four line unit and with frequent combinations. "The Rhyme"
will serve as illustration.

> There is the sign of
> the flower—
> to borrow the theme.
>
> But what or where to recover
> what is not love
> too simply.
>
> I saw her
> and behind her there were
> flowers, and behind them
> nothing. (*For Love,* 23)

Here the stanza is more than regular; each is grammatically complete in itself, a feature found frequently in Creeley's poems of the
early fifties when the stanzas tend to fix themselves on the page with
individual insistence.

In Section Two of *For Love,* the poems of 1956 to 1958, the
quatrain becomes the predominant form, with most stanzas ending
with periods, thus emphasizing again the auditory as well as visible
presence of the stanza unit. Even a poem such as "The Invoice,"
which uses an unusually colloquial diction and syntax, is arranged in
three logical and grammatical units.

> I once wrote a letter as follows:
> dear Jim, I would like to borrow
> 200 dollars from you
> to see me through.
>
> I also wrote another: dearest M/
> please come.
> There is no one
> here at all.

> I got word today,
> viz: hey
> sport, how are you making it?
> And, why don't you get with it. (*For Love*, 86)

As discussed in Chapter 5, Creeley was going through an important period in his life while writing the poems roughly contained in
the second half of *For Love*. His first marriage had ended in 1955;
and early in 1957, he married his second wife, Bobbie. Again as
discussed in Chapter 5, Creeley's poetry reflected this change as it
moved through a bitter skepticism of marriage to a treatment of
woman as mythic muse and, finally, to an acceptance of woman and
the reconciliation of human relationships with poetic production
represented in Bobbie. In a portion of an interview quoted in Chapter 5, Creeley observed that as he personally became more relaxed
his lines became more lyrical; and part of the movement toward a
more lyrical line involved an easing but not an elimination of the
four line stanza. Now the lines lengthened and the syntax tended to
run on from stanza to stanza, resulting in a greater flexibility and
fluidity of line. The effect is not to eliminate the stanza as the
controlling presence but rather to place it in the background,
thereby allowing it to give shape to the poem without obtruding into
it. As Creeley's attitude toward love relaxed, as his lines relaxed, so
did his stanzas. Exceptions remain, of course, but now the stanza
patterns tended to serve not as external skeletons but as internal
skeletons, giving physical shape to the poems without making the
reader so blatantly aware of the form.

The success of this more relaxed pattern can be seen in the
poems, "The Rose" and, particularly, "For Love," discussed in the
conclusion to Chapter 4, but it can be seen in other poems from this
section as well, including "The Name," Creeley's poem to his
daughter by his first marriage.

> Be natural,
> wise
> as you can be,
> my daughter,
>
> let my name
> be in you flesh
> I gave you
> in the act of

loving your mother,
all your days
her ways,
the woman in you

brought from
sensuality's measure,
no other,
there was no thought

of it but such
pleasure all women
must be in her,
as you. But not wiser,

not more of nature
than her hair,
the eyes
she gives you.

There will not be another
woman such as you
are. Remember
your mother,

the way you came,
the days of waiting.
Be natural,
daughter, wise

as you can be,
all my daughters,
be women,
for men

when that time comes,
Let the rhetoric
stay with me
your father. Let

me talk about it,
saving you such
vicious self-
exposure, let you

> pass it on
> in you. I cannot
> be more than the man
> who watches. *(For Love,* 144–45)

Here as in most of Creeley's poetry the insistence is on physical
reality—the name, the act of conception, the child—played off
against the father's rhetoric, ironically, of course, the poem itself.
He is asking that his daughter, "all my daughters," be natural, that
is, complete the forms they are growing toward (as a poem grows
toward its completedness and finally occupies its form), while he,
the father, talks about it and watches. The irony of the poem results
from the child's naturalness opposing the father's rhetoric; however,
through this "rhetoric" the child receives her greatest gift, the
father's love. Although lines are short, the first sentence stretches
out over five quatrains, fifty-eight words followed by the three word
switch, "But not wiser," at the end of stanza five.

As discussed in Chapter 4, Creeley achieved a level of personal
ease during the composition of these late poems in *For Love* with his
marriage to Bobbie, an ease reflected in the integration of myth and
Creeley's own reaction to woman. To this integration must be added
the successful combination of syllable and line on the one hand and a
need for external form on the other. Perhaps this is why many
readers find the poems in the last third of *For Love* among Creeley's
most satisfying.

III   *The Later Poetry*

Creeley's poetry changed during the sixties, of course, and an
important aspect of this change can be seen graphically in a discussion between Creeley and Allan Ginsberg at the Vancouver Poetry
Conference in 1963 and in an epilogue to the published transcript of
that discussion in 1968. In a major section of that transcript Creeley
discussed the literal physical requirement conducive to his act of
composition, insisting that ideally he should have a typewriter (as
opposed to pen or pencil), strong rhythmic music, and paper, usually an 8 x 11 sheet.

I best like, most like, the yellow copy paper that's not spongy, but has a
softness to it, so that when you type, the letter goes in, embeds a little. I

hate a hard paper. When you erase this paper you take a layer off. . . . So I got a legal size sheet. And it was suddenly a terror, because I would finish what was normally my habit of dealing with the paper and realize that I had about six inches left at the bottom that was blank. This set up a whole different feeling.[11]

Creeley did not simply drop a casual remark in the midst of other ideas; this was the point he was making. He was and is acutely aware of the physical context of his own body, and it is not stretching the point to suggest that the same temperament that needs a prescribed physical surrounding for composition also composes poetry and fiction that need external forms.

At the time of this dialogue, however, Creeley's poetry—the poetry of the last part of *Words* and most of *Pieces*—was becoming more and more jagged and elliptical as he attempted to freeze a moment in the fixed frame of the poem. As discussed earlier, particularly in Chapter 2, such an attempt must fail, but the effort as a whole need not fail since each poem contributes to the perception of what is being attempted. In his epilogue to the discussion with Ginsberg, written in 1968, Creeley described how he consciously attempted to move away from those physical conditions described in the dialogue by writing in notebooks. He hoped to achieve a greater immediacy by having the poem come where and when it will.[12] Ironically, perhaps this freedom from physical contexts that Creeley sought resulted in one more context that he found useful: the notebook or journal. Particularly in *Pieces,* and most obviously in two recent prose works, *A Day Book* and *Presences,* Creeley uses the form of the journal to give shape to his statements; and because the form is there, his statements are allowed to take on an even greater sense of formless immediacy. In the poems the two, three, or four line stanzas often remain, but now the moment is caught in the act of spontaneous notebook jotting.

The poems of *Words* and *Pieces* have been discussed in earlier chapters; perhaps it is best here to say simply that the journal entry provided an opening up of Creeley's poetry and a relaxation of the impression, if not always the line. Some poems are presented as off-hand remarks (again the fragment): "So tired/ it falls/ apart" (*Pieces,* 48). Other lines suggest casual rumination as the mind wanders over interesting paradoxes:

> Nowhere one
> goes will
> one ever
> be away
> enough from
> wherever
> one was. (*Pieces*, 50)

Even longer, complete poems, however, often use the journal appearance to provide the form for a series of itemlike stanzas.

> Kids walking beach,
> minnow pools—
> who knows which.
>   .
> Nothing grand—
> The scale is neither
> big nor small.
>   .
> Want to get the sense of "I" into Zukofsky's "eye"—a
> locus of experience, not a presumption of expected value.
>   .
> Here now—
> begin!
> . . . (*Pieces*, 68)

The movement is simple: from observation of an event in stanza one to an abstraction based on that event in stanza two to a relevant reference to an external source in stanza three and then to action resulting from the previous sequence in stanza four. Each item is placed carefully in its appropriate form: Stanzas one and two of equal bulk and shape, stanza three relaxing into longer lines, and stanza four blurting out its three words.

Pieces then is, as Denise Levertov suggested, best read as a journal. Although many of the poems were apparently written literally as journal entries, within the context of the present discussion it is the device of the journal that is important because it gave to many of the poems in this volume and, significantly, to the volume itself both the excitement and convincingness of immediate utterance and the fact of preexistent form. In other words, the sense of a physical journal and the literal act of writing in that journal gave to Creeley enough framework so that he could include anything in the volume—even items that appear formless. It is a mistake, therefore, to see Creeley's poetry moving from order to disorder; rather, it must be seen simply as moving to another kind of order.

IV   Presences *as Form*

From early in his career Creeley published his poetry together with paintings or graphics; however, it must be said that the combination of graphic and poetry was more often sympathetic than illustrative; that is, his poems did not comment on or illustrate the paintings (as did Williams' *Pictures from Brueghel,* for instance) but rather paralleled, in tone perhaps, the paintings or graphics used. An early example is *The Immoral Proposition,* published in 1953 with seven drawings by his friend, René Laubrès; and more recent examples are *St. Martin's* (1971) and *Away* (1976), each with a series of monoprints by his wife Bobbie, and the poem "People," published in a separate volume in 1971 with a series of sketches by Arthur Okamura. In this volume, Okamura's sketches depict tiny human figures arranged together into various geometric shapes and patterns or into stylized shapes such as flowers, while the accompanying poem, in short three line stanzas, makes direct and indirect references to them.

In the examples cited, Creeley appears to be using the illustrative matter as a stabilizing element for his poetry, much as he might use a quatrain or any other external form within which and against which his lines work. More recently, however, Creeley has produced a curious piece of prose that mystified a number of people, but that can be understood to some extent at least within the context of this discussion of form. *Presences* was originally written as an accompanying text to a collection of paintings by Marisol, but the text apparently had so little to do with the paintings that the publisher at first refused to use it. In one sense the publisher was correct—the work is not a text for the paintings; in another and more important sense, however, the publisher was wrong, because Creeley is attempting in this prose work what he sees Marisol doing in her paintings—that is, to lock dreamlike experiences on the canvas through crystallized surreal devices. The fact that his images do not correspond to hers and, further, that his words to not gloss her paintings apparently caused confusion in the minds of some readers, but the work becomes accessible if seen from another angle—or perhaps more accurately from two other angles.

First, in regard to Creeley's need for a priori form. The work itself
is divided into five sections with each section subsequently divided
into three parts of approximately 500, 1000, and 1500 words each.
Creeley was interested in a manuscript of approximately 15,000
words and normally thinks in terms of 500 words to the page; therefore, he needed thirty pages of material. Furthermore, he was in-
trigued with the mathematical symmetry of combining these into
groups of a single page, a double page, and a triple page and then
shifting them according to a simple formula as represented on his
title page:

1. 2. 3.
2. 3. 1.
3. 1. 2.
1. 2. 3.
2. 3. 1.   [13]

Creeley was interested in the fact that a diagonal line could be
drawn from right to left through the numbers. This therefore became the principle upon which *Presences* is organized. The form is
blatantly exterior, even formularized; however, the effect is to free
Creeley from form rather than to trap him in it because now that this
need is fulfilled, he can roam where he will, where his mind and
feelings take him.

And this brings us to the second necessary approach to *Presences*.
Creeley's mind and feelings took him in this work back to a persistent preoccupation over the past twenty-five years—a preoccupation that he saw also in Marisol's paintings. Perhaps even more than
before, the insistence in this work is, as he says here, "When I show
myself as I am, I am, I return to reality" (225). Even while moving
through memories of his own past, through personal feelings,
through reactions to ideas, none of which appear to follow a linear
development, all of which appear as almost journallike entries (the
dates of composition are included following various "entries" and
again one is reminded of the journal aspects of *Pieces* and *A Day
Book*), Creeley's thrust is toward the actuality on the page. He
insists throughout on the fact, from the title *Presences* through a
discussion in the work itself: "Human life he had begun to recognize

as an accumulation of persistent, small gestures and acts, intensively recurrent in their need if not, finally, very much more than that. The *ideas* they delighted in, or suffered, however much they did affect the actuality of all, were nonetheless of a very small measure of possibility" (217). He even attempts using words almost abstractly to suggest, but more than that, to *make real* a "presence": "The clock, on the wall, walks to the door. The door, in the wall, walks to the stair. The stair, up the wall, walks to the window, both ways" (187). Creeley here and elsewhere in *Presences* uses the surreal technique of objects melting into other objects (like Dali's clocks) and the cubist device of seeing various planes of an object simultaneously ("both ways"); however—and this is a crucial qualification—Creeley can do this only because he has already established the form. Because the hole is clearly there to be filled and because it is filled with hard facts, "presences," Creeley is in his own mind free to move nonlinearly across the work. Ironically, the very arbitrariness of the form—geometrically arranged units of five hundred words each—releases Creeley to a freedom of movement and development.

The thesis of this chapter—that Creeley is a classicist who has struggled, often successfully, with the projectivist inclination to disregard a priori form—is seen most clearly in the epigraph to *Presences*. Creeley quotes the contemporary painter, Donald Sutherland: "Classicism is based on presence. It does not consider that it has come or that it will go away; it merely proposes to be there where it is" (184). The fact of form is inextricably bound up with other facts of the poem or piece of fiction. Just as the emotion, the object, and the word must be substantial and able to exist as realities on the page, so must the form, the configuration, the field, the grid. Classicism for Creeley, as for Sutherland, is the insistence on the hard presence, one of which is the shape of the work itself. Creeley needs these "presences," which can be, finally, either fact as form or form as fact.

CHAPTER 7

Final Thoughts

TWO important facts of Robert Creeley's work must enter into any tentative placement and assessment. The first fact is the direction of his poetry over the past twenty-five years and the second is his consistent focus on *the thing*. First of all, look at the titles of his collections: *For Love, Words, Pieces, Thirty Things*. This sequence can be seen—and has been seen by some detractors—as a movement away from humanity—from love to things. Creeley is rejecting emotion, people, in favor of poetry as form. His concern is primarily with the presence of words on the page and not with any possible human activity behind those formal arrangements. Although many readers may react legitimately to Creeley's poetry in this way, it is to miss the very human voice behind and in those words. As emphasized often in this study, Creeley has increasingly attempted to capture sharply and intensely a moment's full experience. His hesitancies, his elliptical arrangements, his nonsyntactical arrangements, his rhythms, his lines are all designed to make real and immediate those moments. The poet who wrote painfully of love and loneliness in his first volume is the same poet who writes of the pain and satisfaction of human emotions in his more recent poems.

I Form and the Human

Thirty Things (1974), *Away* (1976), and the final "Recent poems" section of *Selected Poems* (1976), contain poems as stark and as minimal as any Creeley has published. Some seem little more than chance remarks or thoughts, as in the poem "Xmas," which in its entirety reads, "It commonly sings,/ this Christmas";[1] or the cryptic "A": "head of/ the outside/ inside" (41); or "Sick": "Belly's full/ of rubble."[2] Each poem in these later volumes, however, pricks into

awareness the mind of the reader, matched perfectly in the case of
Thirty Things and *Away* by Bobbie Creeley's monoprint distortions;
and, furthermore, most of the poems approach directly and simply
the condition of being alive in a particular time and a particular
place. Such are:

> Hey
>
> Hey kid
> you.
>
> Flesh filled
> to bursting. (*Thirty Things*, 25)

and the first stanza of "Sound":

> Hearing a car pass—
> that insistent distance
> from here to there,
> sitting here. (*Away*, 16)

This is minimal art in the best sense of the word: simple, direct,
elemental; and it need not exclude direct use of recognizably human
elements. In "Photo," Creeley plays off a monoprint on the facing
page in which one image of a woman slowly blurs down the page
into the same image.

> They say a
> woman passes at
> the edge of the
> house, turning
>
> the corner, leaves
> a very vivid sense,
> after her,
> of having been there. (*Thirty Things*, 43)

Both the print and the poem attempt to capture a precise moment,
the moment immediately following the departure of a figure.
Momentarily, the afterimage remains, much as an image remains on
a screen after the television set has been turned off. But in both

poem and print, the afterimage is not on a television set or even a photograph; rather, it is the image remaining in the mind's eye after someone has left—and that is a profoundly human moment combining sorrow and happiness in a mix that cannot be described, only experienced. A poem such as "Photo" uses minimal effects, but in conjunction with easily recognizable images and emotions, which recalls Creeley's successful and still popular poetry of the fifties.

Creeley's most recent poems, especially those collected in *Away*, in many cases continue these old insistences of physical fact, of the reality of the word, of the attempt, doomed but heroic, to fasten on the moment. In fact, if anything, these insistences become even more desperate, resulting in some poems that are inaccessible except on the most visceral level (here again primarily through a physical response to rhythm and sound). Examples include "A Loop," "Here," "Time," and "Backwards";[3] but these responses also work when placed within an overt human context in poems surpassing any Creeley had previously written. Increasingly, Creeley had been experiencing time as flux, an insubstantial reality within which we grasp at moments. That is the overwhelming fact of life—and its dilemma. The river we step into is always the river but never the same river. A poem entitled "Circle" begins a section titled "Water" as follows: "As much to know you,/ love, to witness this changing surface/ from so constant a place" (*Away*, 56) And in another: "The bubble breaking/ of reflecting mirrors./ Water" (*Away*, 45). The insubstantial surface or present attempts, always unsuccessfully, to reflect the fixed form beneath. Again, the old insistence, as in "The Plan is the Body," in which Creeley pounds away at the "pattern," desperately clutching at this fixed thing even while it slips away. Finally, nothing is left except to repeat the title four times, like a bell tolling.

These desperate attempts are human enough, of course, and deadly accurate; but a powerful mix of precision and emotion is attained in several of these final poems collected in *Away*. "Sitting Here" identifies a father's feeling at the separation from his daughter, an identifiable human experience, but also an experience with considerable potential for cheap sentimentality and cliché. Creeley begins by simply naming the place of the poem: "This/ is window, this is/ sitting at table." Easy enough, until he moves to a photograph of his daughter, and then nothing is fixed. She is gone in the sense that the moment cannot be stopped. The tone grows more desperate:

> Because all these things
> passing, changing,
>
> all the things
> coming and going
> inside, outside—
>
> I can't hold them,
> I want to but
> keep on losing them."

And the poem ends with a brilliant use of water imagery, that parallel to the flux of time, except this time literally so as the face in the photograph is blurred with tears, and all because of "this fact of time spinning" (*Away*, 70–72). Sentimentality and cliché are avoided by the precision of the emotion identified and by placing the regret at separation within the larger context of time passing.

But the poem that moves most, perhaps because it combines Creeley's success in minimal art with the human element, is the elegy on the death of his mother: "For My Mother: Genevieve Jules Creeley, April 9, 1887–October 7, 1972." Creeley's own fondness for the poem is underscored by his publishing it as part of a Black Sparrow pamphlet, in both *Away* and *Selected Poems* (one of only two poems so placed), and at the conclusion of an essay published in William Heyen's collection *American Poets in 1976* with a note identifying it "as instance of what I'm now writing, etc."[4] In this poem Creeley has brought all his instruments of precision to bear upon his own response to personal sorrow. The poem is too long to include here in its entirety; however, some sense of its success can be gained through excerpts. The poem begins, of course, with the physical fact of his mother's life.

> Tender, semi-
> articulate flickers
> of your
>
> presence, all
> those years
> past
>
> now, eighty-
> five, impossible to
> count them

> one by one, like
> addition, sub-
> traction, missing
>
> not one.[5]

The combination of human emotion, the moment impossible to attain, and the difficulty of utterance are all contained, perfectly, in
those first three words: "Tender, semi-/articulate flickers." Even the
sounds play off in two different directions: the internal rhyme of
ar*tic*ulate and f*lick*ers attracting and the awkward consonant
grouping repelling. Ease and difficulty are held in tension throughout the poem. The physical presence of those eighty-five years—see
it as 85 with the final half circle at the end of the 5—metamorphose
into the woman's position on the hospital bed, "curled up,"
supplemented by the hard facts of "hair/ wisped up/ on your head, a/
top knot, body/ skeletal," the curving continuing.

The middle part of the poem focuses on the moment as the moving edge of time. Here we are and there we go, simultaneously:
"sweet flesh caught/ at the edges,/ dignity's faded/ dilemma." This
edge, which is both an end and a continuation is further suggested
by the image of waves breaking in the darkness.

>   Look
> at them, catching
> the light, white
> edge as they turn—
>
> always again
> and again.

This is the flicker, as the semiarticulate follows. It is difficult to say
what he feels, but for Creeley that difficulty is felt physically, as
always.

>   I feel
> the mouth's sluggish-
> ness, slips on
> turns of things
> said, to you,
>
> too soon, too late.

The poem concludes, fittingly, with a modest consolation, con-
centrating on the paradox of the circle, which continues forever but
always comes back to the beginning. His mother's death completes

the cycle of her life; he has returned to see her "one/ last/ time," and his life continues her life and will duplicate it as it duplicates all life with his own return to the beginning, death. As the first few lines set up perfectly and simply the course of the poem, so the last few lines conclude in full: "I am here,/ and will follow." The poem deals with both physical presence and the wisp of time, and the consolation for the mother's death is achieved because of this duality. The son following of the last line is both the son following the mother in death and the son following the mother in life, as life always follows death.

The poem is typical of Creeley's best in the tightly controlled subtlety of the statement, a control achieved through careful technique. First of all, the physical fact of the word ("semi-articulate flicker" is an audio presence) both gives concreteness to a Creeley poem and, what is equally important, allows contrasting general words and phrases to suggest something of their original usage. Here as elsewhere Creeley manages "lovely" and "I love you," but only because they rest on the firm foundation of fact.

Here too is the form of the stanza, the short triplets that give order to the page, a comfortable path along which the poem proceeds rather than a tunnel with hard sides. This is not so much form as the sense of form. The appeal to the subconscious is not on the level of the divine trinity, but rather on the level of pattern. We as Creeley respond to the need for shape provided by the triplet.

But, finally, this poem typifies what Creeley can achieve through the modulated pacing of the lines. Creeley's halting hesitancies, that true modesty so much admired, is accomplished again through the short lines, through the manipulation of end stops that force a pause even though the sense says go on, and through the "scoring" of the punctuation, especially commas. A poem such as "For My Mother" gives a consistently halting impression, but actually the rhythms run from a lunging effect felt almost kinesthetically by the reader to an easy, almost relaxed tempo. The former can be seen in the opening lines quoted above where thoughts are completed not just on the following line but on the first line of the following stanza, the "dropping down" producing physical stumbling, and can also be seen in these lines near the end of the poem:

> and we
> came back

>   to see you one
>   last
>   time, this
>
>   time?[6]

"One last time" are words found on separate lines, and "time" is repeated, this time in the next stanza. Interspersed among these typical Creeley lines are smoother, more relaxed lines, which allow a modulation corresponding to the poet's dual response to his mother's death. The description of his mother is given with a degree of comfort, the syntactical units matching the line breaks, but the feeling of relaxation, even acceptance, is produced by those two final, simple lines referred to earlier: "I am here,/ and will follow." Each unit occupies the line with no sense of clash or discomfort. The consolation is supported at this point by the poem's rhythm.

The easy integrity of this poem reflects Creeley's complete control over his material, but the poem works well because he has combined this technical mastery with an element not always found in his poetry, or at least not found to this extent and this visibly—the human element.

II   Creeley and the American Grain

The other fact of Creeley's poetry is equally simple and equally important, and that is the insistence on the physical reality of the object in the poem. One need only note that the vast majority of poems written by Creeley have titles composed of "The" followed by a noun. This noun may be a concrete object or a human emotion, but whatever is in that poem takes a shape and a substance of its own, thereby requiring no justification beyond its own presence on the page. That fact has been thoroughly discussed and illustrated in this study; nothing more need be said about it except this: such a concern for "the palpable," in Whitman's words, places Creeley squarely within a major tradition of American literature, what some observers take to be the most significant, uniquely American tradition.

Chapter 2 presented Creeley within the Pound-Williams-Olson Projectivist tradition of twentieth century poetry—and examined his poetry as it was similar to and differed from the poetry of that tradition. Appropriately, William Carlos Williams demonstrated the concern of the longer American tradition in his historical study called *In the American Grain* in which he decided to bypass the second-hand commentators on the American experience and go straight to the first-hand sources. As he said in an epigraph to the work, "I have sought to re-name the things seen"[7] because these original observers described the things seen. It has been fashionable throughout much of this century to see the development of American literature in terms of the great unseen—Puritanism, Transcendentalism, Democracy, loss of innocence, power of blackness—but a more important concern than any of these has been the acute awareness of the physical, from the earliest observers of our eastern shore to our young contemporary writers. The early explorers continually noted the forests, the harbors, the kinds of fish and furs available, the habits of the natives; even an observer such as William Bradford, who saw everything as part of God's plan, came back constantly to a physical awareness of things.

And so it continued throughout our literature. The great "Transcendental" writers of the nineteenth century, swimming with heads just barely above the Kantean-Carlylean waters, nevertheless kept an eye fixed on the empirical fact. Thoreau's transcendent symbol of the pond, which gives him back the image of his own soul, is measured accurately and in minute detail by this surveyor of land. Throughout *Walden*, the physical detail is looked at as with scientific instruments, and Thoreau never can leave this world for some other. Even *Moby Dick*, that most confounding of books, which treats Ishmael's journey as mankind's journey and the great white whale as a perplexing symbol piled on symbol, is first of all, and perhaps most impressively of all, a reconstruction of whaling in nineteenth century America. Detail after detail, fact after fact, in all their convincing literalness are piled high until the reader has had the actual adventure itself, has smelled and felt and tasted. And Whitman, too, lists object after object, people, places, trees, parts of the body, in order to suggest what is America. The list goes on. Hawthorne and Poe, most affected by the Gothic supernatural, never can accept total separation from the necessities of this world. Hawthorne insists that his story of Hester really was discovered in a customhouse and gives us a long, introductory account of that discovery; and Poe never describes a supernatural event without making known the possible, natural explanation for that event: perhaps the wind blew the curtains.

And on into this century, when the poetic revolution of the teens and twenties arose in some sense from the fact becoming literal once again. The Imagists, product of many forces and personalities, focused on the thing; Robert Frost told of New England objects. Even Eliot, product of his own admiration for the French Symbolistes, came down, at least early, on the thing, the wet streets, the sawdust floors. And then, too, Williams ("No Ideas but in Things") and the Projectivist preoccupation with the literal utterance of the word. My point in this brief survey is that Creeley belongs squarely in the tradition described here. As he himself observed, "My 'saints,' then, are those men [Columbus, Poe, Whitman, Pound, Hart Crane] who defined for me an explicit possibility in the speech that I was given to use, who made the condition of being American not something chauvinistically national but the intimate fact of one life in one place at one time."[8] Furthermore, a case could be made, indeed has been made by Williams and others, that Creeley's is the most uniquely American tradition.

And, finally, Creeley sees "New Englandly." In many ways, the American poet of the last century most like Creeley is Emily Dickinson: both are private individuals who wrote of themselves intimately and at times cryptically. Both attempt to capture the moment between heartbeats or—more accurately for Dickinson—the moment after the final heartbeat. And both use short, elliptical, often breathless lines. But beyond that, a New England poet, as Creeley understands and as Frost so perfectly demonstrates, inherits a *way* of speaking. Growing up in New England, Creeley said, gave him "that sense of speech as a laconic, ironic, compressed way of saying something to someone. To say as little as possible as often as possible."[9] New England history causes one to watch his words carefully; perhaps even New England geography contributes. People who have had to scrape out a living from the rocky soil of coastal New England know the value of conserving—conserving effort and conserving words. Constant preoccupation with the land produces a respect for it certainly, but beyond that it produces an awareness that the land is constantly there. So too with words. As the mass of words is reduced, the single word becomes more significant, perhaps even more real. This, too, is a fact of Creeley's poetry and his fiction and a fact of America's literature.

Robert Creeley then is both a New England poet and an American poet in fundamental ways. While associated with avant garde developments in the poetry of the last twenty-five years and while attesting personally in various places to the impact of Pound's title, *Make It New,* Creeley must also be seen as a part of a vital, ongoing tradition in American literature.

III *Assessment*

Any assessment of Robert Creeley is both premature and presumptuous. He is in midcareer, undoubtedly with major work yet to come; in fact, when reading through his poetry especially, one gets the impression that all this is but preparation. Any assessment, therefore, would have to be decidedly tentative. Presumptuous, too, because quite simply he can do things with words that most people, including this writer, cannot do. I have, however, read and reread carefully and thoughtfully all of his words that I could locate, and I have read everything again written about him that I could locate, so perhaps that entitles me to a few rash comments.

First of all, I believe that Creeley's major accomplishment will be technical and that he will be remembered primarily as a craftsman. Time and again I have been impressed with the total control he exerts over the rhythms, especially, of his prose and poetry. The line, the pauses, the hesitancies, the syntax and ellipses usually mirror precisely the statement of the poem; in fact, in his best poems and in his best short stories, these elements become the statement itself. What he says is relatively less important than how he says it, or at least I believe that that is what future generations will say. He does, however, say something about his world, and for a number of reviewers, while that world may be void of values, "a shattered world," in the words of Allen B. Cameron, "in which all sense of values is lost," the poems for many readers and, again, for Cameron, "attempt to give order and value to at least one moment of experience."[10] Ellen Maslow is even more emphatic in her defense of Creeley's statement: "Creeley is finding the new life in homilies. He has the courage to discover simplicity, and to firmly guide his readers toward what is, in fact, wholesomeness. He is existentially affirmative, believes in love which has been stripped of the myths of love. He is not facing a void, and is not afraid of the Twentieth Century. His poems express a calm he has acquired by accepting limitations."[11] Nevertheless, I believe that Creeley's major accomplishment has been not in what he has said, important

and useful though that statement may be, but in the way he has
said it.

Second, Creeley has chosen, or as he might say, it has been
chosen for him, to write poetry that constricts itself to a small point
of intensity, with the emphasis on small as well as intensity. His
poetry and fiction avoid the grand statement and the grand method;
in fact, they accept technical limitations in the same way that they
accept thematic limitations. His work is minimal in that it functions
more by what is excluded than by what is included. The question
then is not so much whether Creeley is or will be known as a major
writer, but rather whether minimal art itself can ever be major. In
other words, has Creeley, by the course he runs, removed himself
from consideration as a major writer? Although any answer to this
question can be argued endlessly, I suspect that the answer is yes.
So far in his career at least, Creeley's work lacks both the thematic
and technical scope to qualify as major. Within the self-imposed
limitations of his poetry and fiction, the achievement is impressive;
however, those self-imposed limitations are still limitations. To the
literary historian, that evaluation is both justifiable and understand-
able; however, to the poet such a statement remains fortunately
irrelevant.

My third observation is even more personal. Although I think that
Creeley will continue to be known primarily as a poet, I prefer the
short stories, and this despite the fact that no new stories have
appeared since "The Book" appeared in *Evergreen Review* in 1961.
For me the short story form itself is long enough for Creeley to
develop a discernible shape and to allow the impulse generating that
story to become accessible to the reader, while at the same time it is
short enough to allow the sustaining of a moment in time. More
completely than in anything else he has written, the "point" of a
short story is the form that it takes, justifying nicely his statement
that "form is what happens." Individual poems approach this
method, but the poems taken as a whole, especially the later ones,
are more valuable for what they attempt than for what they achieve.
Indeed, my point throughout most of the discussion of the poetry
has been that the achievement has been in the attempt. As I indicated in the chapter on Creeley's fiction, his novel failed as form; it
became finally a sequence of individually realized parts rather than a
satisfying completion in itself. Creeley's more recent prose pieces,
A Day Book and *Presences*, are interesting and even intriguing, but

I think useful only in where they will finally lead. I look forward to following Creeley's attempt to carry out his effort to discover a fictional form consistent with his own demands, although I cannot help but wish that he could return to the earlier stories. But, of course, he cannot. He too is trapped by "that damn history again, the chronological."[12]

Finally, what is Creeley's position in the larger context of his contemporaries? What does he offer them? What do they take? When reading what others have said about Creeley, I have been struck by the respect, admiration, and even love found in their words, especially those of other poets and most especially those of younger poets. From the early days when he corresponded with Pound (the courage must have come from ignorance) and Charles Olson, Williams, and Robert Duncan, Creeley's words have been listened to. Olson quoted this brash young poet in his influential essay on "Projective Verse," and Creeley himself gave both a forum and a direction to the poetry emerging in the early fifties in his *Black Mountain Review*, primarily a product of his own taste and judgment. Today young poets quote him almost as much as he continues to quote Williams and Olson. His readings are always crowded with students, who respond to the unpretentious, unassuming sight of this man speaking honestly and directly about himself and then reading his own insistent poems, punctuating each line with his voice, even with his own body. He strikes the reader and viewer as totally open and totally honest about himself, about his poetry, and about his feelings.

Notes and References

Preface

1. "Introduction to Charles Olson II," *A Quick Graph: Collected Notes And Essays* (San Francisco: 1970), p. 188.
2. " 'For Love' of," *Kulchur*, II (Winter 1962), p. 54.

Chapter One

1. "Why Bother," *A Quick Graph*, p. 40.
2. The most useful biographical sources for Creeley are Mary Novik, "A Creeley Chronology," *Athanor*, IV (Spring 1973), 67–75; John Sinclair and Robin Eichele, "An Interview with Robert Creeley," *Whe're* 1 (Summer 1966), 45–58, reprinted in Robert Creeley, *Contexts of Poetry: Interviews 1961–1971* (Bolinas, Cal., 1973), pp. 45–69; and "Lewis MacAdams and Robert Creeley," in *Contexts of Poetry*, pp. 137–70 (hereafter cited as MacAdams).
3. MacAdams, p. 138.
4. Sinclair and Eichele, p. 45.
5. MacAdams, p. 148.
6. *Ibid.*, p. 149.
7. Sinclair and Eichele, p. 46.
8. *Ibid.*, p. 48.
9. *Ibid.*, p. 50.
10. *Ibid.*, p. 49.
11. *Ibid.*, p. 51.
12. Novik, p. 68.
13. *Ibid.*, p. xiii.
14. "Linda W. Wagner: A Colloquy with Robert Creeley," in *Contexts of Poetry*, p. 82.
15. Michael André, "Michael André: An Interview with Robert Creeley," in *Contexts of Poetry*, p. 194.
16. In June 1977 Robert Creeley married Penelope Highton of New Zealand.
17. Wagner, "A Colloquy", p. 78.
18. "The New World," *A Quick Graph*, p. 207.
19. M. L. Rosenthal, "The 'Projectivist' Movement: Robert Creeley,"

The New Poets: American and British Poetry Since World War II (New York, 1965), pp. 151–57.

20.   "A Note on Ezra Pound," *A Quick Graph*, p. 95.

21.   "Introduction to *The New Writing in the USA*," *A Quick Graph*, p. 44.

22.   "Introduction to Charles Olson: *Selected Writings II*," *A Quick Graph*, p. 185.

23.   "Charles Olson: *Y & X*," *A Quick Graph*, p. 151.

24.   "A Note on Ezra Pound," *A Quick Graph*, p. 96.

25.   William Carlos Williams, *In the American Grain* (New York, 1956), p. 133.

26.   William Carlos Williams, *The Selected Letters of William Carlos Williams*, ed. John C. Thirwell (New York, 1957), p. 130.

27.   "A Note on the Local," *A Quick Graph*, p. 34.

28.   "The Fact," *A Quick Graph*, p. 117.

29.   "Introduction to *The New Writing in the USA*," *A Quick Graph*, p. 50.

30.   "Robert Creeley in Conversation with Charles Tomlinson," *Contexts in Poetry*, p. 15.

31.   Williams, *Selected Letters*, p. 321.

32.   *Whitman* (Harmondsworth, Middlesex, England, 1973), pp. 13–16.

33.   Linda W. Wagner, "An Interview with Robert Creeley," *The Minnesota Review*, V (October-December 1965), 316.

34.   In "Introduction to *The New Writing in the USA*," Creeley summarized what he looked for in the work he selected: "That understanding most useful to writing as an art is for me, the attempt to *sound* in the nature of the language those particulars of time and place of which one is a given instance, equally present" (*A Quick Graph*, p. 52).

35.   "Edward Dorn in the News," *A Quick Graph*, p. 216.

36.   Wagner, "An Interview," p. 320.

37.   Charles Olson, "Projective Verse," in *Poetics of the New American Poetry*, ed. Donald Allen and Warren Tallman (New York, 1973), p. 149. Compare Ernest Fenollosa's insistence on the transitive verb in *The Chinese Written Character As a Medium for Poetry*, edited by Ezra Pound (San Francisco, 1936), p. 13.

38.   *Ibid.*, p. 148. Olson acknowledges in his essay that this statement was taken from Creeley, who expressed it at other times. For instance, after discussing James Joyce's stylistic innovations as evolving out of the statement, he said in a 1951 essay, "Form is the extension of content" ("Notes for a New Prose," *A Quick Graph*, p. 12).

39.   *Ibid.*, p. 151.

40.   *Ibid.*—

41.   *Ibid.*, 150–51.

42. *Ibid.*, p. 152.

43. Compare Williams' essay, "The Poem as a Field of Action," *Selected Essays* (New York, 1969), pp. 280–91: "Where else can what we are seeking arise from but speech? From speech, from American speech as distinct from English speech, or presumably so, if what I say above is correct. In any case (since we have no body of poems comparable to the English) from what we *hear* in America" (p. 290).

44. Part II of the essay was not discussed here. Olson makes some observations on "the degree to which the projective involves a stance toward reality outside a poem as well as a new stance toward the reality of a poem itself" (p. 155) and concludes with a criticism of T. S. Eliot as a nonprojective—i.e., intellectual only—poet.

45. "A Note on Poetry," *A Quick Graph*, p. 26.

46. "Paradise/ Our/ Speech . . . ," *A Quick Graph*, p. 124.

47. Wagner, "An Interview," p. 311.

48. "Louis Zukofsky: 'A' *1–12 & Barely and Widely*," *A Quick Graph*, p. 122.

49. In 1960 Donald Allen included ten poets in the Black Mountain section of *The New American Poetry: 1945–1960* (New York, 1960): Olson, Robert Duncan, Denise Levertov, Paul Blackburn, Creeley, Paul Carroll, Larry Eigner, Edward Dorn, Jonathan Williams, and Joel Oppenheimer, noting in his preface that Blackburn, Carroll, Eigner, and Levertov had no ties with the college itself (p. xii).

50. Linda Wagner and Lewis MacAdams, 'The Art of Poetry X," *Paris Review*, XI (Fall, 1968), 155–87, in Robert Creeley, *A Sense of Measure* (London, 1973), p. 86

51. Something of the importance of the *Black Mountain Review* to young nonestablishment poets can be seen in the statement made by Joel Oppenheimer in a review of the reprint of the *Review* published in 1969: "It is difficult to remember the isolation a writer such as myself felt in the fifties. The sense, the absolute insistence upon the fact, that one had no peers that were of use or interest seemed depressingly clear. There were magazines, of course; they made the young writer even more depressed. Not only was there no hope of being represented in their pages, but that writer whose learning had come from the tradition of Williams and Pound knew that his work, scattered and inchoate, had no relation to the narrowly conceived policies of these respected journals . . . . How fantastic it was, then, to see the *Black Mountain Review*: a journal that not only presented the work of men who shared one's concerns, but that established a ground on which the American writer could stand" (*Poetry*, CXVI [May, 1970], 110–11).

52. Martin Duberman, *Black Mountain: An Exploration in Community* (Garden City, New York, 1973), p. 433.

53. Wagner, "An Interview," p. 321,

54. Sinclair and Eichele, p. 49.

55. *Ibid.*, p. 47.

56. "Preface to *All That Is Lovely in Men*," *A Quick Graph*, p. 4.

57. *Contexts of Poetry*, pp. 49–50.

58. MacAdams, p. 153.

59. "Robert Creeley in Conversation with Charles Tomlinson," *Contexts of Poetry*, p. 25.

60. MacAdams, p. 156.

61. Wagner, "A Colloquy," p. 124.

Chapter Two

1. *Pieces* (New York, 1969), p. 49. Further references will be given in the text.

2. Louis L. Martz, "Recent Poetry: The End of an Era," *The Yale Review*, LIX (Winter 1970), 261.

3. Denise Levertov, "What Made the Shadows Darker," *Caterpillar*, 10 (January 1970), 246.

4. Charles Potts, "*Pieces:* The Decline of Robert Creeley," *West Coast Review*, V (April 1971), 5.

5. Daniel Hughes, *Massachusetts Review*, XI (Autumn 1970), 654.

6. Reed Whittemore "*Pieces* by Robert Creeley," *New Republic*, CLXI (October 11, 1969), 25.

7. Martz, p. 259. See also the review of the separate 1968 publication of *Numbers* by Gil Sorrentino, *Poetry*, CXVI (May 1970), 110–14.

8. Russell Banks, "Notes on Creeley's *Pieces*," *Lillabulero*, 8 (Winter 1970), 88–91.

9. Levertov, p. 246.

10. *Words* (New York, 1967), p. 9.

11. All poems are titled in the Table of Contents; however, one cannot help but wonder just how much this is a publisher's convenience.

12. "Was That a Real Poem or Did You Just Make It Up Yourself?" in *American Poets in 1976*, edited by William Heyen (Indianapolis, 1976), p. 49 (hereafter cited as "Was That . . .").

Chapter Three

1. "The New World," *A Quick Graph*, p. 207.

2. *Words*, p. 22. Further references will be given in the text.

3. Thomas A. Duddy, "On Robert Creeley," *Stony Brook*, 3/4 (1969), 385.

4. "A Note," *A Quick Graph*, p. 32.

5. John Thompson, "An Alphabet of Poets," *New York Review of Books*, XI (August 1, 1968), 35.

6. Ronald Hayman, "From Hart Crane to Gary Snyder," *Encounter*

XXXVII (February 1969), 77.

7. Peter Davison "New Poetry: The Generation of the Twenties," *Atlantic Monthly*, CCXXI (February 1968), p. 141.

8. John Perreault, "Holding Back and Letting Go," *New York Times Book Review*, November 19, 1967, p. 97.

9. Louis Simpson, *Harper's Magazine*, CCXXXV (August 1967), 90.

10. G. S. Fraser, "A Pride of Poets," *Partisan Review*, XXXV (Summer 1968), 474–75.

11. Donald Junkins, *Massachusetts Review*, IX (Summer 1968), 598, 601.

12. Duddy, p. 387.

13. Frederic Will, "To Take Place and to 'Take Heart,' " *Poetry*, CXI (January 1968), 257.

14. "Poems Are a Complex," *A Quick Graph*, p. 54.

Chapter Four

1. Peter Davison, "The New Poetry," *Atlantic Monthly*, CCX (November 1962), 85.

2. Paul Carroll, "Country of Love," *Nation*, CICV (August 25, 1962), 78.

3. D. J. Hughes, *Massachusetts Review*, IV (Spring 1963), 607.

4. Ralph J. Mills, *New Mexico Quarterly*, XXX (Summer 1960), 197.

5. Colin Falck, *Encounter*, XXVIII (March 1967), 68.

6. Robert Duncan, *New Mexico Quarterly*, XXXII (Autumn/Winter 1962–63), 219–24.

7. Stanley Kunitz, *Harper's Magazine*, CCXXV (October, 1962), 103.

8. Frederick Eckman, "Six Poets, Young or Unknown," *Poetry*, LXXXIX (October 1956), 60.

9. *For Love: Poems 1950–1960* (New York, 1962), p. 31. Further reference will be given in the text.

10. Mary Novik, in *Robert Creeley: An Inventory, 1945–1970* (Kent, Ohio, 1973), was able to date most of these poems with considerable precision from the typescripts at Washington University and Indiana University. I have relied on her for all composition dates mentioned hereafter.

11. David Ossman, *The Sullen Art* (New York, 1963), pp. 59–60.

12. Allen B. Cameron, " 'Love Comes Quietly': The Poetry of Robert Creeley," *Chicago Review*, XIX, ii (1967), 94.

13. Duncan, p. 221.

14. *Ibid.*, p. 223.

15. "The Fascinating Bore," *A Quick Graph*, p. 255.

16. Robert Graves, *The White Goddess, A Historical Grammar of Poetic Myth* (New York, 1948), p. 449.

17. Charles Altieri, in a perceptive article called "The Unsure Egoist: Robert Creeley and the Theme of Nothingness," also sees Creeley coming to a resolution in Bobbie, but he goes on to point out that "Creeley had

conceived of Bobbie and the home she made possible as permanent peace outside the flux of time, but he soon realized that real peace must be found within, not beyond, the flux." *Words* begins Creeley's search within himself for an answer to the void (*Contemporary Literature*, XIII [Spring 1972], 172).

Chapter Five

1.   Warren Tallman, "The Writing Life," in *New American Story*, edited by Donald M. Allen and Robert Creeley (New York, 1965), p. 4.

2.   Complete composition and publication dates for these stories appear in Novik, *Inventory*, pp. 80–82.

3.   Wagner, "An Interview with Robert Creeley," p. 314.

4.   *The Gold Diggers and Other Stories* (New York, 1965), p. 314.

5.   *Ibid.* Further references will be given in the text.

6.   Wagner and MacAdams, pp. 155–87.

7.   Anthony Keller, *Commonweal*, LXXXIII (December 10, 1965), 319.

8.   Samuel Moon, "Creeley as Narrator," *Poetry*, CVIII (August 1966), 341.

9.   Warren Tallman's essay, "Robert Creeley's Rimethought," was originally published in *Tish* (January 4, 1966), pp. 2–10; then in *A Nosegay in Black*, I (Autumn 1966); and finally in *Three Essays on Creeley* (Toronto, 1973). Despite being published three times, this article, as many articles on Creeley, is in very limited circulation.

10.   Bernard Bergonzi, "Out Our Way," *New York Review of Books*, V (January 20, 1966), 22.

11.   Saul Maloff, "Of Life and the Living," *New York Times Book Review*, November 7, 1965, p. 60.

12.   D. J. Enright, "Manner Over Matter," *New Statesman*, LXX (August 6, 1965), 188.

13.   Moon, p. 342.

14.   The original working draft of *The Island* is at Washington University and includes the dates of its composition. The working draft contains the completion date of January 6, 1963. Mary Novik (*Inventory*, p. 157) includes a reference to "With two drafts of the ending, the second completed February 20, 1963."

15.   *The Island* (New York, 1963), p. 35. Further references will be given in the text.

16.   Recall Creeley's observation to David Ossman (p. 60) after his marriage to Bobbie that "as I begin to relax . . . the line can not so much grow softer, but can become, as you say, more lyrical, less afraid of concluding."

17.   *A Day Book* (New York, 1972), p. 58. Further references are given in the text.

18.   Creeley used a variation of the journal in *Presences: A Text for*

Marisol, which is discussed in Chapter 6.

Chapter Six

1. Robert F. Kauffman, "The Poetry of Robert Creeley," *Thoth*, II (Winter 1971), 31.
2. C. Bowen [Carl Harrison-Ford], "A Continuity, A Place—The Poetry of Robert Creeley," *Poetry Magazine* (Australia), XVIII (October 1970), 9.
3. Olson, "Projective Verse," p. 148.
4. *Whitman*, p. 15.
5. "I'm Given to Write Poems," *A Quick Graph*, p. 72.
6. "A Sense of Measure," in *A Sense of Measure*, p. 33.
7. Robert Frost, "The Figure A Poem Makes," in *American Poetic Theory*, edited by George Perkins (New York, 1972), pp. 209–10.
8. "A Sense of Measure," *A Sense of Measure*, p. 32.
9. "Notes Apropos 'Free Verse,' " *A Quick Graph*, p. 59.
10. "Was That A Real Poem . . .," p. 49.
11. "Contexts of Poetry," *Audit*, V (Spring 1968), 5.
12. *Ibid.*, p. 17.
13. "Presences, A Text for Marisol," *Io*, 14 (Summer 1972), 183. Further references are given in the text and are to this edition. *Presences* (New York, 1976).

Chapter Seven

1. *Thirty Things* (Los Angeles, 1974), p. 37. Further references are given in the text.
2. *Away* (Santa Barbara, 1976), p. 69. Further references are given in the text.
3. *Selected Poems* (New York, 1976), p. 171, 180. Further references are given in the text.
4. "Was That a Real Poem," p. 53.
5. "For My Mother: Genevieve Jules Creeley: April 9, 1887–October 7, 1972," *Sparrow* 6 (March 1973), [10].
6. *Ibid.*, [p. 13].
7. Williams, *In the American Grain*, p. v.
8. "I'm Given to Write Poems," *A Quick Graph*, p. 69.
9. Ossman, p. 63.
10. Cameron, p. 94.
11. Ellen Maslow, "A Discussion of Several of Creeley's Poems," *Kulchur*, 20 (Winter 1965–66), 67.
12. *A Day Book*, p. 58.

Selected Bibliography

A more complete, though not annotated, bibliography of secondary sources may be found in Mary Novik's *Robert Creeley; An Inventory, 1945–1970*. Montreal: McGill-Queen's University Press, 1973. The Primary Sources listed below are taken from this Inventory and are augmented with Creeley's post-1970 publications.

PRIMARY SOURCES

Le Fou. Columbus, Ohio: Golden Goose Press, 1952.

The Kind of Act Of. Palma de Mallorca: The Divers Press, 1953.

The Immoral Proposition. Karlsruhe-Durlach, Germany: Jonathan Williams, 1953.

The Gold Diggers. Palma de Mallorca: The Divers Press, 1954. *The Gold Diggers and Other Stories*. London: John Calder, 1965. *The Gold Diggers and Other Stories*. New York: Charles Scribner's Sons, 1965. *De goudgravers en andere verhalen*. Amsterdam: Olak & Van Gennep, 1966. *El Amante Y Otros Cuentos*. Editorial Letras, 1967.

A Snarling Garland of Xmas Verse. Palma de Mallorca: The Divers Press, 1954.

All That Is Lovely in Men. Asheville, North Carolina: Jonathan Williams, 1955.

If You. San Francisco: The Porpoise Bookshop, 1956.

The Whip. Worcester, England: Migrant Books, 1957.

A Form of Women. New York: Jargon Books, 1959.

Four Poems from "A Form of Women." New York: Eighth Street Bookshop, 1959.

For Love: Poems 1950–1960. New York: Charles Scribner's Sons, 1962.

The Island. New York: Charles Scribner's Sons, 1963. *The Island*. London: John Calder, 1964. *Die Insel*. Frankfurt am Main: Insel, 1965.

Distance. Lawrence, Kansas: Terrence Williams, 1964.

Two Poems. San Francisco: Oyez, 1964.

Mister Blue; Sechzehn Geschichten. Frankfurt am Main: Insel, 1964.

Words. Rochester, Michigan: The Perishable Press, 1965. *Words*. New York: Charles Scribner's Sons, 1967. *Gedichte*. Frankfurt am Main: Suhrkamp, 1967.

149

New American Story. Ed. with Donald Allen. New York: Grove Press, 1965.
About Women. Los Angeles: Gemini, 1966.
Poems 1950–1965. London: Calder and Boyars, 1966.
For Joel. Madison, Wisconsin: The Perishable Press, 1966.
A Sight. London: Cape Goliard Press, 1967.
Robert Creeley Reads. London: Turret Books/ Calder and Boyars, 1967.
The Finger. Los Angeles: Black Sparrow Press, 1968.
5 Numbers. New York: The Poets Press, 1968. *Numbers*. Stuttgart: Edition
    Domberger; Dusseldorf: Galerie Schmela, 1968, *NUMBERS: A Se-
    quence for Robert Indiana*. New York: The Poets Press, 1968.
The Charm: Early and Uncollected Poems. Mt. Horeb, Wisconsin: The
    Perishable Press, 1967. *The Charm: Early and Uncollected Poems*. San
    Francisco: Four Seasons Foundation, 1969.
The New Writing in the U.S.A. Ed. with Donald Allen. Harmondsworth,
    Middlesex, England: Penguin, 1967.
The Boy. Buffalo, New York: The Gallery Upstairs Press, 1968.
Divisions & Other Early Poems. Mt. Horeb, Wisconsin: The Perishable
    Press, 1968.
Pieces. Los Angeles: Black Sparrow Press, 1968. *Pieces*. New York: Charles
    Scribner's Sons, 1969.
Mazatlan: Sea. San Francisco: Poets Press, 1969.
Hero. New York: Indianakatz, 1969.
A Quick Graph: Collected Notes & Essays. San Francisco: Four Seasons
    Foundation, 1970.
Mary's Fancy. New York: Bouwerie Editions, 1970.
In London. Bolinas, California: Angel Hair Books, 1970.
The Finger: Poems 1966–1969. London: Calder and Boyars, 1970.
For Betsy and Tom. Detroit: The Alternative Press, 1970.
For Benny and Sabina. New York: Samuel Charters, 1970.
As Now It Would Be Snow. Los Angeles: Black Sparrow Press, 1970.
Christmas: May 10, 1970. Buffalo, New York: The Lockwood Memorial
    Library, State University of New York at Buffalo, 1970.
St. Martin's. Los Angeles: Black Sparrow Press, 1971.
A Day Book. New York: Charles Scribner's Sons, 1972.
Listen. Los Angeles: Black Sparrow Press, 1972.
"Presences, A Text for Marisol," *Io*, 14 (Summer 1972), 183–226. *Presences:
    A Text for Marisol*. New York: Charles Scribner's Sons, 1976.
Whitman. Ed. and Introduction by Robert Creeley. Harmondsworth,
    Middlesex, England: Penguin Books, 1973.
A Sense of Measure. London: Calder and Boyars, 1973.
Contexts of Poetry: Interviews 1961–1971. Bolinas, California: Four Seasons
    Foundation. 1973.
The Creative. [Sparrow 6]. Los Angeles: Black Sparrow Press, 1973.
Inside Out. [Sparrow 14]. Los Angeles: Black Sparrow Press, 1973.

Thirty Things. Los Angeles: Black Sparrow Press, 1974.
"Was That a Real Poem or Did You Just Make It Up Yourself?" [Sparrow
40]. Los Angeles: Black Sparrow Press, 1976. Also in William Heyen,
ed. *American Poets in 1976*. Indianapolis: The Bobbs-Merrill Company, Inc., 1976.
Away. Santa Barbara: Black Sparrow Press, 1976.
Selected Poems. New York: Charles Scribner's Sons, 1976.

SECONDARY SOURCES

ALTIERI, CHARLES. "The Unsure Egoist: Robert Creeley and the Theme of
Nothingness." *Contemporary Literature*, XIII (Spring 1972), 162–85. A
perceptive examination of Creeley's poetry as it wrestles with the pro-
blem of the void. Especially valuable in relating Creeley's poems to
contemporary philosophy.
ALEXANDER, MICHAEL. "William Carlos Williams and Robert Creeley."
Agenda, IV (Summer 1966), 56–67. Urges British readers and poets to
take Williams and Creeley seriously.
ANDRÉ, MICHAEL. "Two Weeks with Creeley in Texas." *Chicago Review*,
XXIV, 2 (1972), 81–86. Notebooklike appreciation of Creeley.
BOWEN, C. [CARL HARRISON-FORD] "A Continuity, A Place—The Poetry
of Robert Creeley." *Poetry Magazine* (Australia), XVIII (October 1970),
3–9. An introduction to readers in Australia.
BROWNJOHN, ALAN. "Some Notes on Larkin and Creeley." *Migrant*, 6
(May 1960), 16–19. Contrast between "Days" by Philip Larkin and "I
Know a Man" by Creeley.
CAMERON, ALLEN B. *Canadian Forum*, XLVII (August 1967), 117–18. Con-
tends that with *Words* "Creeley has . . . unquestionably established
himself as a major poet."
———. " 'Love Comes Quietly': The Poetry of Robert Creeley." *Chicago
Review*, XIX, ii (1967), 92–103. A valuable article based primarily on an
examination of *For Love*.
CARROLL, PAUL. "Country of Love." *Nation*, CICV (August 25, 1962),
77–78. A perceptive review of *For Love*.
———. "The Scene in the Wicker Basket." In *The Poem in Its Skin*,
pp. 31–38. Chicago: Follett Publishing Company, 1968. A psychologi-
cal reading of "The Wicker Basket," "this good hip poem."
CHUNG, LING. "Predicaments in Robert Creeley's *Words*." *Concerning
Poetry*, II (Fall 1969), 32–35. Argues that Creeley's awkwardness re-
sults from a " 'baby-walk' style of perceiving as well as his struggle to
fill the words."
CLAYRE, ALASDAIR. "The Rise and Fall of Black Mountain College." *The
Listener*, March 27, 1969, pp. 411–14. Discussion of the history of
Black Mountain College, including among others Olson and Dorn.

COLLINS, DOUGLAS. "Notes on Robert Creeley." *Lillabulero*, II (Winter 1968), 27–40. Favorable review of *Words*.

CORMAN, CID. " 'For Love' of." *Kulchur*, II (Winter 1962), 49–64. Favorable early essay on Creeley's poetry.

———. *Poetry*, LXXXIII (March 1954), 340–42. Close analysis of the title poem from *The Kind Of Act Of* to demonstrate the subtlety and intricacy of Creeley's poetry.

COX, KENNETH. "Address and Posture in the Poetry of Robert Creeley." *Cambridge Quarterly*, IV (Summer 1969), 237–43. The posture is "first person speaking to second (mute) with awareness of unknown third."

CRUNK, ———. [ROBERT BLY] "The Work of Robert Creeley." *The Fifties*, 2 (1959), 10–21. While praising Creeley's pre–*For Love* poems, he also notes that the American poetic tradition itself is not rich enough to sustain great poetry.

DAVEY, FRANK. "Black Days on Black Mountain." *Tamarack Review*, 35 (Spring 1965), 62–71. Defense of Black Mountain influence on Canadian literature and an account of Black Mountain's most important features and its poetic antecedents.

DAVISON, PETER. "New Poetry: The Generation of the Twenties." *Atlantic Monthly*, CCXXI (February 1968), 141–42. Creeley's *Words* announces "the victory of the inarticulate."

———. "The New Poetry." *Atlantic Monthly*, CCX (November 1962), 85–86. Sees Creeley working in *For Love* toward his own original style.

DEMBO, L. S. *Conceptions of Reality in Modern American Poetry*. Berkeley: University of California Press, 1966. Contains a chapter, "Postscript: Charles Olson and Robert Duncan; The Mystique of Speech and Rhythm."

DORN, EDWARD. *Caterpillar*, 10 (January 1970), 248–50. Cryptic praise in a review of *Pieces*.

DUBERMAN, MARTIN. *Black Mountain: An Exploration in Community*. Garden City, New York: Anchor Books, 1973. An excellent account of the rise and fall of Black Mountain College with considerable information concerning Creeley's relationship to it and his stay there.

DUDDY, THOMAS A. "On Robert Creeley." *Stony Brook*, 3/4 (1969), 385–87. Useful review of *Words*.

DUNCAN, ROBERT. *New Mexico Quarterly*, XXXII (Autumn/Winter 1962–63), 219–24. Discussion of *For Love* within the tradition of love poetry.

ECKMAN, FREDERICK. *Cobras and Cockle Shells: Modes in Recent American Poetry*. Flushing, New York: Felix Stefanile/Sparrow Magazine, 1958. Early volume on Creeley's generation.

———. "Six Poets, Young or Unknown." *Poetry*, LXXXIX (October 1956), 60–62. Perceptive review of *All That Is Lovely in Men*.

EICHELE, ROBIN. "The Berkeley Poetry Conference." *Work*, 2 (Fall 1956), 73–79. Journal response to the conference where Creeley read his lecture, "A Sense of Measure," and conducted a seminar.

ENRIGHT, D. J. "Manner Over Matter." *New Statesman*, LXX (August 6, 1965), 187–88. Mixed review of *The Gold Diggers* praising Creeley's skill at handling language and wondering if it is all worth it.

FLES, JOHN. "The Root." *Kulchur*, I (Spring 1960), 39–42. Responds to Creeley's emphasis on the physical presence of the thing.

FLINT, R. W. *The New York Review of Books*, I (November 14, 1963), 10. Review of *The Island*, which sees the novel as "a happy marriage of 'New England' conscience . . . to Beat ambitions."

FRANKS, DAVID. *Whe're*, 1 (Summer 1966), 94–96. Favorable review of *The Gold Diggers*, emphasizing the self-sufficiency of the stories.

FULLER, JOHN. *London Magazine*, VI (November 1966), 107–108. Negative review of *For Love*, referring to Creeley's love poetry as "skinny Thurber."

GUNN, THOM. "Things, Voices, Minds." *Yale Review*, LII (Autumn 1962), 129–38. Brief mention of Creeley in terms of the influence of Williams and his tie to the Elizabethans.

HAMMOND, JOHN G. "Solipsism and the Sexual Imagination in Robert Creeley's fiction." *Critique*, XVI, iii (1975), 59–69. Examines Creeley's fiction as it wrestles with the conflict of withdrawing into the self or establishing a relationship, the failure of the latter presented in terms of sexual failure.

HAYMAN, RONALD. "From Hart Crane to Gary Snyder." *Encounter*. XXXII (February 1969), 72–79. Criticizes *Poems 1950–1965* because of lack of substance and the mannered effect.

HICKS, GRANVILLE. "The Poets in Prose." *Saturday Review*, LXVIII (December 11, 1965), 31–32. Favorable review of *The Gold Diggers*, preferring it to *The Island*.

HOWARD, RICHARD. *Alone with America: The Art of Poetry in the United States Since 1950*. London: Thames and Hudson, 1970. Pp. 65–70. An examination of *For Love* and *Words*.

HUGHES, D. J. *The Massachusetts Review*, XI (Autumn 1970), 652–55. Generally unfavorable review of *For Love*, although he finds in the final section some "spiritual progress and an increasing desire actually to make complete poems."

JONES, LE ROI. *Kulchur*, 3 (Summer 1961), 81–83. Praise for *A Form of Women*, saying that it must be read intently but it is worth the effort.

JUNKINS, DONALD. *Massachusetts Review*, IX (Summer 1968), 598, 601. In this favorable review of *Words*, Junkins points out that Creeley is writing about poetry with his two main themes being measure and proportion.

KAUFMAN, ROBERT F. "The Poetry of Robert Creeley." *Thoth,* II (Winter 1971), 28–36. Discusses Creeley's Projectivist Verse in terms of its parallel to quantum physics and wave mechanics.

KUNITZ, STANLEY. *Harper's Magazine,* CCXXV (October 1962), 103, 108. In a review of *For Love* he calls Creeley the best of a school of "actualists"—those determined to record the fact strictly and sparely.

LEVERTOV, DENISE. "What Makes the Shadows Darker." *Caterpillar,* 10 (January 1970), 246–48. Perceptive review of *Pieces.*

MARTZ, LOUIS. "Recent Poetry: The End of an Era." *Yale Review,* LIX (Winter 1970), 252–67. Favorable review of *Pieces* with special emphasis on "Numbers."

MASLOW, ELLEN. "A Discussion of Several of Creeley's Poems." *Kulchur,* 20 (Winter 1965–66), 66–71. Argues against the contention that Creeley is a nihilist.

McGANN, JEROME. "Poetry and Truth." *Poetry,* CXVII (December 1970), 195–203. A highly favorable review of *Pieces* with the emphasis on the integrity of individual poems and the unity of the volume.

MESSING, GORDON. "The Linguistic Analysis of Some Contemporary Nonformal Poetry." *Language and Style,* II (Fall 1969), 323–29. Discussion of the difficulty of applying linguistic analysis to modern colloquial poetry using Creeley's "I Know a Man" as one of three examples.

MOON, SAMUEL. "Creeley as Narrator." *Poetry,* CVIII (August 1966), 341–42. Perceptive comment on the stories of *The Gold Diggers* as they concern human relationships.

NOVIK, MARY. "A Creeley Chronology." *Athanor,* IV (Spring 1973), 67–75. A short but detailed biographical sketch.

———. *Robert Creeley: An Inventory, 1945–1970.* Kent, Ohio: The Kent State University Press, 1973. An exhaustive listing of primary and secondary sources.

OLSON, CHARLES. "Introduction to Robert Creeley." In *Human Universe and Other Essays,* pp. 127–28. San Francisco: Auerhahn, 1965. Reprint of early appreciation of several Creeley stories that were published together with this essay in *New Directions,* No. 13 (1951).

OPPENHEIMER, JOEL. "The Inner Tightrope: An Appreciation of Robert Creeley." *Lillabulero,* 8 (Winter 1970), 51–53. A personal reflection on the "perilous journey" of Creeley's poetry.

OSSMAN, DAVID. *The Sullen Art.* New York: Corinth Books, 1963. Contains Creeley's first interview.

PAUL, SHERMAN. "A Letter on Rosenthal's 'Problems of Robert Creeley.' " *Boundary,* II (Spring 1975), 747–60. Excellent defense of Creeley's journal method in *Pieces* and *A Day Book.*

ROSENTHAL, M. L. *The New Poets: American and British Poetry Since World War II.* New York: Oxford University Press, 1967. Contains a chapter on "The 'Projectivist' Movement," with twelve pages on Creeley.

SAROYAN, ARAM. "Extension of Content." *Poetry,* CIV (April 1964), 45–47. Highly favorable review of *The Island,* examining the novel as it relates to Creeley's poetry.

SIMPSON, LOUIS. *Harper's Magazine,* CCXXXV (August 1967), 89–90. Review of *Words* in which he sees these poems primarily in terms of style.

SORRENTINO, GIL. "Black Mountaineering." *Poetry,* CXVI (May 1970), 110–20. Discussion of Creeley's importance as editor of *Black Mountain Review.*

STEPANCHEV, STEPHEN. *American Poetry Since 1945.* New York: Harper and Row, 1965. Contains a chapter on "Projective Verse" with six pages on Creeley.

TALLMAN, WARREN. *Three Essays on Creeley.* Toronto: Coach House Press in Association with Beaver Kosmos, 1973. A reprint of three excellent essays: "Robert Creeley's Rimethought," "Robert Creeley's Portrait of the Artist," and "Robert Creeley's *The Island.*"

TOMLINSON, CHARLES. (ed.). "Robert Creeley in Conversation with Charles Tomlinson," *The Review: A Magazine of Poetry and Criticism,* 10 (January 1964), 24–35. Also contains an anthology of Black Mountain poetry edited by Tomlinson, plus "Notes on Poetics: Regarding Olson's 'Maximus'," by Robert Duncan, and a brief introduction, "Black Mountain as Focus," by Tomlinson.

WAGNER, LINDA. *Critique,* VII (Spring 1964) 119–22. Review of *The Island* with emphasis on techniques common to both Creeley's poetry and his fiction.

———. *Studies in Short Fiction,* III (Summer 1966) 465–66. Brief examination of *The Gold Diggers* as it reflects Creeley's difference from other contemporary fiction writers.

WHITTEMORE, REED. "*Pieces* by Robert Creeley." *New Republic,* CLXI (October 11, 1969), 25. A negative review of *Pieces,* calling it a preaching book hiding behind an antipreaching pose.

WILL, FREDERIC. "To Take Place and to 'Take Heart.'" *Poetry,* CXI (January 1968), 256–58. Sees *Words* as a group of poems hovering on the point of just having been made.

"A Workable Bibliography of Robert Creeley." *Whe're,* 1 (Summer 1966), 58–60. Includes the order of composition of poems since *For Love.*

ZUKOFSKY, LOUIS. "What I Come to Do Is Partial." *Poetry,* XCII (May 1958), 110–12. Brief, favorable review of *The Whip.*

Index

(The works of Creeley are listed under his name)